Endorsements

"This beautifully crafted collection of scriptures offers readers a profound way to connect with God. As you journey through the pages, you'll find yourself reflecting on moments of joy, hope, and possibilities. Whether you are seeking comfort during difficult times or looking to deepen your faith, this book provides a companion for every season of life. It is a powerful tool for reflection, connection, and it has the potential to inspire a deeper relationship with God. Used properly, secrets from heaven will be revealed."

—**Stephie Young**, Vice President, Advanced Meeting Solutions

"The chapter 'Secrets to Applying God's Wisdom to Your Life' is not only compelling but inspiring. This chapter discusses the story of Daniel and his unwavering confidence in God. His story serves as an inspiration to those seeking God's wisdom. If you're searching for spiritual guidance and a closer relationship with God, this book is a must read. Latanya challenges her readers to think about their relationship with God. After reading this chapter, I have completely reexamined my faith in God."

—**Michelle Burton**, Student, Ohio Christian University

"Latanya's book, *When God is First Secrets from Heaven are Revealed, a Sequel*, delivers a divine perspective on how God is dependable to help his people in desperate times of need. In reviewing this book, the attention paid to detail allows the reader to easily follow the evolution of Daniels victory. The construction of the book mirrors well with the lifestyle of Daniel, the Bible, and lends itself successfully to the study of that time period in biblical history. This book is an excellent resource for faith building. Latanya is a proven author with her book *Secrets from Heaven* and now the creditable follow-up with this new work."

—**Lawana Christian**, MSW, LSW, LICDC

"Understanding the story of Esther in Latanya's new book puts the journey of finding your purpose in perspective. The trials and tribulations that Esther went through to identify and meet her purpose are similar to what we as individuals must endure to understand God's purpose for us. Esther's story connects the Bible to real life, proving that God is always with us no matter what happens in life."

—**Neta Cason**, Director, US Planning Abbott Nutrition

When God Is First Secrets from Heaven Are Revealed,
a Sequel

When God Is First Secrets from Heaven Are Revealed

A SEQUEL

Pray and Expect an Answer!

Latanya M. Hughes

RESOURCE *Publications* · Eugene, Oregon

WHEN GOD IS FIRST SECRETS FROM HEAVEN ARE REVEALED, A SEQUEL
Pray and Expect an Answer!

Copyright © 2025 Latanya M. Hughes. All rights reserved. Except for brief quotations in critical publications or reviews, no part of this book may be reproduced in any manner without prior written permission from the publisher. Write: Permissions, Wipf and Stock Publishers, 199 W. 8th Ave., Suite 3, Eugene, OR 97401.

Resource Publications
An Imprint of Wipf and Stock Publishers
199 W. 8th Ave., Suite 3
Eugene, OR 97401

www.wipfandstock.com

PAPERBACK ISBN: 979-8-3852-4425-6
HARDCOVER ISBN: 979-8-3852-4426-3
EBOOK ISBN: 979-8-3852-4427-0

VERSION NUMBER 05/27/25

Scripture quotations are taken from Holy Bible, New International Version®, NIV® Copyright ©1973, 1978, 1984, 2011 by Biblica, Inc.® Used by permission. All rights reserved worldwide.

Contents

Acknowledgments | vi
Introduction | vii

Chapter 1: Secrets Are Revealed in Prayer | 1
        Power Points on Receiving Secrets in Prayer

Chapter 2: Secrets to Having Faith in God | 15
        Power Points on Having Faith in God

Chapter 3: Secrets to Knowing God's Purpose for Your Life | 28
        Power Points on Knowing God's Purpose for Your Life

Chapter 4: Secrets to Applying God's Wisdom to Your Life | 59
        Power Points on Applying God's Wisdom to Your Life

Chapter 5: Secrets to Waiting on God | 75
        Power Points to Waiting on God

Bibliography | 87

Acknowledgments

Thank You

To my amazing mother for her faith, tenacity, and the endless support she has given me. Her resilience and persistence has inspired me to keep going, no matter what I face. My heart overflows with gratitude for my beautiful mother, a gift from the Lord that I will cherish forever. I love you Mom!

With Love and Appreciation

To my family and friends, your unwavering support and love hasn't gone unnoticed. Thank you for giving me the courage to embrace my God-given purpose.

Introduction

This is what the Lord says, he who made the earth, the Lord who formed it and established it—the Lord is his name: "Call to me and I will answer you and tell you great and unsearchable things you do not know."

—Jeremiah 33:3

After I published my last book, *Secrets from Heaven*, I was instructed by the Lord to write another book. The Lord said, "*Secrets from Heaven* only scratched the surface of my intended message to my people." In other words, the Lord is urging believers to pursue a closer relationship with him. When you read your Bible, you will notice that our Lord is always inviting us to have intimate conversations with him. By engaging in intimate conversations and meditating on the Scriptures, we can strengthen our relationship with God. As we grow closer to him, we can freely express our fears, dreams, and concerns. By sharing our emotions and experiences with God, we will receive comfort, strength, and the guidance we need.

INTRODUCTION

When we approach God, expressing our most intimate thoughts, the Bible reminds us in Jeremiah 29:12 that God is listening. That's right; the Lord hears everything we say. The Lord will also teach us how to hear his voice, which is the best part about spending time with him. Our ability to recognize the Lord's voice and understand his will is critical. For this reason, it's important to seek God's counsel. According to Proverbs 29:18, when there is no vision and no guidance from God, people perish. Yet, when we learn to listen to the Lord's voice, this allows us to connect with him on a deeper level. Therefore, let us cultivate the art of listening and God will reveal his secrets to us.

Do you have a desire to know what God is thinking? I do. First Corinthians 2:16 says, "We have the mind of Christ." Since the Spirit of God lives in us, we are given knowledge of God's plans. The Holy Spirit will help us discern between right and wrong, and as a result, we can make decisions that reflect God's will. Yet, to know the mind of God will require trusting him. Do you trust God? If not, what has caused your lack of faith in God? Consider what the Lord says about you in John 15:15. The Lord calls you a friend. Therefore, the Lord will share with you everything the Father tells him. In fact, the Lord will share his secrets with you because he can trust you. The Lord knows he can depend on you to make a significant impact on his kingdom.

Furthermore, I am confident that the Lord led me to write *When God Is First Secrets from Heaven Are Revealed, a Sequel* as evidence that he doesn't hold any secrets from us. Within my new book, there are several chapter titles that are repeated from the first book, like "Prayer, Faith, and Wait." While the chapter titles remain the same, the text is updated and filled with valuable information. By the end of these chapters, you will realize God has a plan for us, and only those who actively seek him will uncover the hidden secrets.

I am also excited to introduce to you two new chapters titled "Secrets to Knowing God's Purpose for Your Life" and "Secrets to Applying God's Wisdom to Your Life." The purpose of these two chapters is to help you discover how important it is to collaborate

INTRODUCTION

with the Lord. As you collaborate with the Lord, you will learn how to align your thoughts and actions with his will. By seeking guidance through prayer and Scripture, we can better understand what the Lord desires from us. When we have God's wisdom, we can fulfill our purpose, which is our kingdom assignment. Think on this: because you are created in Christ's image, you have the capacity to be brilliant. Therefore, the Lord will help you think outside the box and give you creative solutions to solve any problems. However, you must be determined, resilient, and unstoppable about pursuing your God-given purpose.

In addition, each chapter ends with Power Points to help you stay motivated to make a difference in God's kingdom. The Power Points also include Bible verses that relate to each chapter. The Power Points can also be used as a resource for daily meditation and prayer to help you grow spiritually. I pray this will make your experience of learning your Bible more enjoyable and effective.

A final note, I hope you enjoy the written words in this book from God to you. As I continue to seek God, I have discovered that putting him first gives us access to his secrets. Unlocking God's secrets is a lifelong journey that requires commitment to him. By making God a number-one priority, our lives are meaningful, purposeful, and fulfilling. So let us give God the honor that he truly deserves.

1

Secrets Are Revealed in Prayer

Jabez cried out to the God of Israel, "Oh, that you would bless me and enlarge my territory! Let your hand be with me, and keep me from harm so that I will be free from pain." And God granted his request.

—1 Chronicles 4:10

Jabez, a Descendant from the Tribe of Judah

JABEZ WAS A MAN with wisdom who passionately pursued the Lord. The Bible records in 1 Chronicles 4:9 that he was more righteous than all his siblings. Jabez was also a descendant from the tribe of Judah. Judah was the fourth son of Leah and Jacob, the Hebrew patriarch. According to Genesis 29:35, when Leah gave birth to her son Judah, she said, "This time I will praise the Lord." Sadly, Leah was not satisfied despite having three sons who were older than Judah, whose names were Reuben, Levi, and Simeon.

Leah was more concerned with pleasing her husband than praising the Lord for her other sons. She had children for the wrong reasons because she desperately wanted her husband's love. Do you remember a time when you didn't acknowledge the Lord's blessings as Leah did? How often do you praise the Lord for bestowing his favor upon you? Think about this: if Christ didn't do anything else for us, surely, we should accept his decision. The very fact that Christ died on the cross for the sins of the world should be enough for all of us (John 3:16). When we understand how much God loves us, our hearts are filled with gratitude and our praise is never-ending. With this in mind, when we praise the Lord, we are acknowledging that he deserves to be glorified and honored.

Furthermore, the tribe of Judah, also known as the royal bloodline, brought forth great kings like David and Solomon. While both kings made a tremendous impact on God's kingdom, the greatest king that ever lived is Jesus Christ. The Savior of the world, Jesus Christ can be traced back to the Judaic lineage, according to Matthew 1:1-17. Among the tribes of Israel, Judah is the most powerful and popular tribe. In addition, Jacob, Judah's father, states in Genesis 49:9–10 that the name "Judah" is symbolic of a fearless lion. Jacob also declared that no one would bother Judah because of his strength, leadership, boldness, fierceness, and his peaceful spirit. These great qualities that Judah possessed were also passed down to another man of God, Jabez.

Jabez, a Praying Man Labeled at Birth

Jabez realized how blessed he was to inherit such brilliant attributes from his ancestors. Therefore, the man of God didn't allow his surroundings to keep him from living a purpose-filled life. For instance, when Jabez was born, his mother suffered a great deal while giving birth. Because of this, 1 Chronicles 4:9 reads, his mother named him Jabez, meaning "sorrowful." Although given this label by his mother, Jabez became a natural-born leader. Despite the negative connotation of his name, he achieved great things in life. His resilient attitude is an excellent example of how we can do remarkable things for Christ despite our upbringing. Have your childhood or adulthood experiences prevented you from fulfilling your God-given purpose? Oftentimes, negative stereotyping will hinder you from reaching your divine purpose. Unfortunately, in life, all of us have experienced some bad moments. Yet, when we have faith in the Lord, we understand that our bad experiences have a purpose. It is through our experiences that the Lord will develop, mold, and shape us into the person he wants us to be.

Even if we have suffered pain, the Lord can still touch us where the pain exists, but we must accept his healing hands. His healing power is endless and will mend our deepest wounds. Proverbs 4:22 confirms that God's word has the power to heal and restore us. Isn't it wonderful to know that we can turn to the Scriptures for comfort and strength in our most difficult times? Within this text, the author boldly proclaims that God's word is like medicine to the entire body. This Scripture offers encouragement for those in search of healing and spiritual renewal. Therefore, we must take time to study and understand our Bible. As we do this, we will experience both physical and spiritual healing. That being said, the Holy Scriptures are more than just a collection of words on a page—they're a powerful resource that we should read every day. Consider this: if we have a desire to grow spiritually, we need to read God's word. When we read our Bible, we are reminded that we have access to God's divine wisdom and guidance. The wisdom of God empowers us to make informed decisions and follow his will. Now then, let us embrace the healing power of God's Holy Scriptures, which will transform, rebuild, and revitalize us.

With this in mind, we are assured in Romans 8:28 that the Lord will turn all our suffering into something good. Having said this, the Lord's intentions are to bless you and not harm you. His precious thoughts toward you are pure and pleasant. In fact, Jeremiah 29:11 says the future that God has planned for you is filled with love, peace, and joy. This great news should give you a new perspective on how much God loves you. Knowing that you are precious to God should motivate you to do his will with joy and enthusiasm. Every believer should be involved in building up God's kingdom. When we are more concerned about the things of God, we won't lack anything. Receiving this revelation should ignite your spirit and give you a passion to fulfill your purpose.

Jabez Wanted Unlimited Business Opportunities

Moreover, Jabez knew the importance of staying focused on the Lord to accomplish his divine purpose. Primarily, the man of God acknowledged that the Lord created both heaven and earth. Thus, nothing on this earth is sustained without God. As a man who revered God, Jabez knew he needed God's approval on every endeavor. Instead of asking his family and friends' opinion, Jabez spoke with God about his business ventures. In 1 Chronicles 4:10, we learn that Jabez asked the God of Israel to bless and expand his business opportunities beyond his local community. As an entrepreneur, Jabez wasn't concerned about the what-ifs, maybe, or failures. He was primarily focused on having unlimited business prospects. Jabez's vision of having unrestricted business possibilities would allow him to build and grow God's kingdom. More importantly, with God's wisdom, Jabez would have divine strategies on how to be successful. This same truth applies to us; when we allow God to broaden our thinking pertaining to his kingdom, prosperity is certain.

Do you believe that the Lord has given you tremendous power, dominion, and influence to rule over regions? If you have an entrepreneurial mindset, you can create innovative products and services for God's kingdom. Your God-inspired, state-of-the-art products could possibly span across the world. Having said this, are you ready to receive a global ministry? When you study the Bible, you will find that Jesus's ministry extended far beyond his place of residence. With this in mind, what steps are you taking to expand your ministry? Better yet, what about starting a ministry in your hometown? Whether your ministry is local or global, the Lord has commanded believers to tell everyone about eternal salvation (Matthew 28:16–20). When we share the gospel, 1 Timothy 2:4 records, the Lord is pleased because he wants everyone saved. As Christians we must inform our family, friends, and strangers about Christ's forgiveness of sins. By sharing the good news of Jesus Christ, we are inviting others to experience his love and grace. Taking this into consideration, let's take advantage of every opportunity to share our faith with everyone we meet. Therefore, let us be bold, compassionate, and vigilant in our sharing the gospel, knowing that every opportunity is a precious one.

Jabez Asks for God's Protection

Jabez also realized that he needed God's protection. With bold confidence in the Lord Almighty, Jabez prayed and asked for protection from any life-threatening situations as he went into unfamiliar territory. The man of God understood Psalm 91:1-2, which says we will have security and peace of mind when we put our complete trust in the Lord. Proverbs 18:10 also describes the name of the Lord as a mighty shield of strength and protection. Keeping this in mind, the Lord is a safe haven for the righteous. As we bask in the Lord's presence, we will experience his love and peace. While this is true, one must ask, why is it so hard for believers to rest in God's presence? Having said this, when was the last time you rested in the Lord's gentle arms? If it's been a while, it's time to prioritize your spiritual wellbeing so you can feel his warm embrace again. Perhaps resting in the arms of God is difficult for you. Consider what John 14:27 says: the Holy Spirit's peace resides in you. Since you are filled with the Holy Spirit, instead of letting your concerns burden you, accept God's peace. Resting in his loving arms is indeed a beautiful feeling that can only be experienced by those who know him. Given what has been said, how well do you know your Father, God? Imagine this: when you truly get to know God, you will see that he cares about every detail of your life. Therefore, you will rest in his loving arms because you know that in him, you find comfort, support, and protection. That being said, resting in his arms is a place of peace, and there is no better place to rest.

Further, as you fulfill your kingdom assignment, you can be certain that the Lord will protect you. When your enemies try to attack you with discouragement and fear, look to God. The resurrected Jesus Christ has all power over your enemies. In fact, Psalm 110:1 says be still because the Lord has promised to put your enemies under your feet. No matter how challenging things may appear, this Scripture serves as a reminder that we are never alone. Therefore, with the Lord's help, you are not defeated but victorious over the enemy's tactics. With this knowledge, you can rest assured that any weapon formed against you will not prosper because the Lord is your vindicator (Isaiah 54:17). Now then, hold onto God's promise and believe what he said.

God Grants Jabez's Request

Furthermore, Jabez had tremendous faith in the Lord. He was certain that the Lord would always listen to him. What about you? When you pray, are you doubtful or certain that the Lord hears you? Throughout your Holy Bible, the Lord clearly says that he will listen and answer his children. Isaiah 65:24 says it best: even before we ask, the Lord will answer our prayers. First Chronicles 4:10 is another powerful reminder that our prayers and petitions are heard by a loving and caring God. The text says, "Jabez cried out to the God of Israel, 'Oh, that you would bless me and enlarge my territory!'" After hearing Jabez's heartfelt prayer, the Lord gave him what he desired. Jabez's prayer reveals that we too can receive an answer from the Lord by engaging in sincere, heartfelt worship. As we pray and wait like Jabez did, we can be confident that an answer is soon to come.

God Desires to Hear Our Voice

Then Jesus told his disciples a parable to show them that they should always pray and not give up.

—*LUKE 18:1*

Our loving Father God, who adores his children, is eager to fellowship with us. God, the life-giver to mankind, intentionally created us to seek him. Although some people assume that God isn't near them, in fact, he is much closer than they think. Therefore, God is more visible to us as we become in tune with his presence. As we acknowledge God's presence, we will encounter him in everyday life. That said, we are told throughout the sacred Scriptures, especially in Acts 17:27, that God is waiting for us to find him. Being mindful of this, Deuteronomy 4:29 also says seeking the Lord passionately will lead us to him. With this mind, we are all given access to know the Lord personally. Once the Lord is found, we will develop an authentic and personal relationship with him. Taking this into account, we should be excited about the opportunity to commune with the Lord. After all, our faith is strengthened when we deliberately look for him. The experience of communing with the Lord will be extraordinary and transformative. Being open to receiving God's wisdom can change our lives. Having said this, as we approach the Lord with enthusiasm and reverence, divine insight is revealed. Given that we have divine insight, we now have the privilege to understand the mind of God. Knowing the mind of God allows us to please our Lord.

Prayer Creates Intimacy with God

The importance of prayer is further emphasized by Jesus in Luke 18:1. Within this passage, Jesus is teaching a parable about prayer to his disciples. Jesus begins the parable by telling his disciples to pray without ceasing. This same parable still applies today. By praying consistently, we can avoid disappointment, worry, and hopelessness. More importantly, when we purposefully pray, we are motivated by the Lord to keep praying. Besides, the act of praying intentionally creates moments of intimacy with God. For instance, having a close relationship with God allows us to express our deepest feelings. During this time, personal information is exchanged between you and God.

    Needless to say, building a relationship with God will not happen overnight. Think about it: getting to know a person doesn't happen instantly either. Relationships are established by spending time together. Wouldn't you agree? That being said, we should always focus on building a better relationship with God. How can we say we love the Lord when we don't have a relationship with him? Are you interested in knowing the Lord? Making God a priority will lead to a deeper relationship with him. As you learn how to trust the Lord, you will have peace, guidance, and a sense of purpose in your life. With God's wisdom, you will understand his will for your life. By following God's guidance, you will make better decisions that align with his purpose. Living a life of purpose brings great joy and fulfillment to your life.

Wait to Hear from God

Furthermore, having a prayer life will also teach us how to wait on God's response. However, waiting on God will require patience. When our lives are led by the Spirit of God, we are not anxious; rather we are joyful while we wait on God. Although waiting is critical, you should always expect an answer from God. Just because God hasn't responded doesn't mean that he isn't listening. At times, waiting on an answer from God may seem tiresome or challenging. Nonetheless, Isaiah 40:31 points out that our strength is restored when we wait, expect, and have hope in God. We are reminded in Galatians 5:22 that all believers are filled with patience, which is a characteristic of the Holy Spirit. We can also learn about the spirit of patience in Ecclesiastes 7:8, which says, "The end of a matter is better than its beginning, and patience is better than pride." To put it another way, despite life's ups and downs, we must trust God and endure to the end. For example, situations that we are experiencing may not look promising at first. Yet, with patience, along with an expectant attitude, the end result is favorable.

Further, Paul enlightens the church by saying in Philippians 4:6, "Don't worry about anything; instead, pray about everything. Tell God what you need, and thank him for all he has done" (NLT). By telling believers not to worry, Paul is saying we shouldn't get discouraged but keep praying until God answers. Think about this: when you pray and read your Bible, it's impossible for the enemy to infiltrate your mind with discouragement.

Having said this, your prayers are not forgotten but delayed until a specific season. Please remember, the Lord is never late; rather, he is always right on time. Rest assured, God isn't avoiding you. The Lord can be trusted; therefore, hold on to the promises of God. Remain faithful, be patient, and always rely on God. As you do this, your faith and your persistent attitude will be remembered in the eyes of the Lord.

The Widow's Persistent Faith

Let's finish reviewing the prayer parable taught by Jesus in Luke 18:1-5. A persistent widow is mentioned in this text to illustrate that a prayer life is necessary for Christians. The widow in the story is seen as being persistent and committed to receiving justice. She repeatedly pleaded with the town judge for protection from her enemy. Yet, the unjust judge lacked empathy and showed no concern for the widow's mental state. Because the judge was aware that the woman was overwhelmed and a widow, he had a responsibility to help her. According to Psalm 9:9, the Lord is a place of refuge for the poor and their helper in times of trouble. Also, in Deuteronomy 27:19, the Lord will curse anyone who fails to fight for a widow's rights. In ancient times, widows were viewed as powerless, oppressed, and less fortunate than others. For this reason, without hesitation, the judge should have assisted the widow. Although the judge refused to act upon what was just and fair, the widow was adamant in her pursuit for justice. The widow wasn't worried about bothering the judge. With that said, her unwavering attitude left a lasting impression on the judge. With a determined spirit, the widow got on the judge's nerves. Finally, the widow's relentless behavior caused the judge to give in to her demands.

People Will Be Lovers of Themselves

After reading Luke 18:4, did you notice the judge confessing that he doesn't fear God? I did. Do you think the judge's statement reflects the current state of today's society? Unfortunately, we are raising a generation that doesn't know God. Sadly, there is a lack of reverence for God in our society. The absence of spiritual values is the reason why we have become a godless nation. Our nation has become what 2 Timothy 3:2 says: people are not only selfish but are arrogant, disrespectful, ungrateful, love money, and live unholy lives. The sad truth in today's world is that many people do not love God or their neighbors. The lack of love for God will cause people within a nation to lose self-control and exhibit unrestrained behavior.

Proverbs 25:28 says it best by providing an excellent illustration of what our nation is like. The Scripture reveals that a person without self-control is like a city whose walls are broken down. Whenever there is a lack of spiritual guidance, people are cruel, proud, and unforgiving. Their selfish desires are so strong that they are willing to lie, steal, and mistreat others to get what they want. Listen to what Proverbs 14:34 says: sin is a disgrace to a nation, but when people live righteously, the nation is exalted. Sin, however, will always bring God's divine judgement. Now without delay, let us do as 2 Chronicles 7:14 says: repent of our wickedness and return to the Lord. The Lord is willing to forgive us, especially when our apology is authentic. The Lord can reverse his punishment when we admit that we are truly sorry. Keeping this in mind, all men must develop a habit to fear and obey God.

The Power of Persistent Prayers

Moreover, do you have the audacity to be tenacious and determined like the widow woman? Her steadfast faith demonstrates that there is power in having a persistent attitude. The widow's courageous behavior caused her to be victorious over the enemy's tactics. Are you taking a stand against the enemy by continuously bringing your concerns to the Lord? Despite your overwhelming circumstances, the Lord will not abandon you. As a matter of fact, Luke 18:7 clearly says that when we talk to the Lord consistently, he will surely deliver us from our troubles. Since the

Lord is always listening, you should feel inspired to pray. Why? Because prayer changes everything. Having said this, when you pray, are you confident that the Lord hears you? If so, do you believe that your prayers are making a difference? We are assured in the Scriptures that the Lord will always hear our prayers because he cares. Whether we are asking for guidance or strength, our prayers will always reach the ears of our Father. First John 5:14-15 confirms that the Lord is ready to respond, especially when we pray according to his will.

Maybe your faith in prayer is not as strong as it should be. Well, I have great news: having a prayer life is the most powerful weapon that God has given you. Instead of giving up, use your spiritual weapons: your Bible and prayer. Having courage and perseverance are essential for fighting your battles. In utilizing these spiritual tools, you will learn how to fight and win! Now then, stand firm in the Lord. When you do this, the Lord will give you strategies on how to defeat the adversary. On the other hand, you must realize the enemy isn't concerned about your feelings or you. Actually, the devil knows the power you possess. The question is, are you aware of the power that dwells within you? The same power that raised Jesus from the dead is in you! Therefore, if you have lost your power, take it back from the enemy (who, by the way, has none). The enemy only has power because you gave it to him. Unfortunately, if you're not sure that God's power resides in you, then the enemy will stop at nothing to perform his job, which is to steal, kill, and destroy you. Nevertheless, John 10:10 records, Jesus entered the world so that we may have life forever. The abundant life that Christ has given you and I are filled with blessings and power.

Faith is Confidence in God

Furthermore, Psalm 5:12 states that the Lord will protect the upright person and give him favor. A perfect example of this passage is a young man by the name of David who received God's unmerited favor on many occasions. One event in the Bible which is worth reading is the famous story of Goliath and David. Have you read the story of David and Goliath? Just in case you haven't, David was a young man facing a life-threatening situation. Like the widow, David was brave, enthusiastic, determined, and had faith. The first time David met Goliath, the nine-foot-tall soldier, the Philistines and the Israelites were preparing for battle. Right before the battle began, Goliath bullied the Israelites and threatened to kill them. The Israelites and King Saul were horrified when they heard Goliath's harsh words. Filled with fear, 1 Samuel 17:24 tells us that when the Israelites saw Goliath, they immediately ran.

On the other hand, 1 Samuel 17:26–32 says that David was not intimated when he saw Goliath, who was known as a champion fighter. Instead, David said to the Israelites, "Who is this uncircumcised Philistine, who continues to disrespect God's army?" The term "uncircumcised" means a male who isn't circumcised, non-Jewish people, or someone who doesn't believe in God. David called Goliath uncircumcised because he was the enemy, a pagan who didn't believe in God. David, however, with his brave and warrior-like spirit, asks King Saul if he could fight Goliath. David's request was granted. The young warrior was very confident that the all-powerful living God would fight for him. David knew that God would allow him to be victorious over Goliath. Therefore, because of his faith in God, David killed Goliath, as stated in 1 Samuel 17:50.

How are you dealing with the giants in your life today? Consider this throughout your life: challenging situations will always stare you in the face. Sometimes, our trials may appear to be as tall as the nine-foot giant, Goliath. Even a nine-foot giant like Goliath has his weak spots. Notice I said "appear" in the above sentence. In most cases, when you're feeling overwhelmed, nine times out of ten, it's the enemy trying to discourage you. Don't you dare listen to him. Listen to the Lord and don't hesitate to talk to him about your problems. When you partner with God, you will receive strength and strategies to overcome your difficult times. The Lord says in Isaiah 41:13 don't be afraid because he is always available to help you. John 14:27 says the Lord has given you peace; therefore, you are not to be worried or fearful. If you allow God to influence your thinking, you will be transformed from the inside out. Thus, giant situations will become very small when your mind is changed. Even now, you can praise the Lord differently. Seeing life from a different point of view will cause you to be more grateful to God. Suddenly, your eyes are opened and now you realize every battle belongs to God. As a result of this, you believe what Jeremiah 32:27 proclaims nothing is too hard for God! Therefore, you have already won the battle!

Power Points on Receiving Secrets in Prayer

Consistently seeking the Lord's presence is the key to succeeding in your kingdom assignment. Prayer is the fuel that ignites your passion for your assignment. Prayer is also the place where God will reveal how to receive unlimited resources. With endless opportunities, you can be creative and innovative at expanding God's kingdom. When you depend on God, your influence will reach places your mind could never imagine. That being said, if you want to hear God's voice, regular communication with him is essential. Listed below are six Power Points called P.R.A.Y.E.R., which is a reminder that prayer works.

P assion, prayer, persistence, patience, and the Holy Spirit is what you will need to accomplish your assignment. Having a zeal for God will help you gain the confidence you need to be effective in the kingdom. Remember to saturate yourself in God's word. Prayer should also be part of your daily routine (1 Thessalonians 5:16; Jeremiah 17:5–7; Job 42:2; Luke 11:8–10).

R ely on God for divine revelation. When you know the mind of God, navigating your assignment is easier. With prayer and strategies from the Lord, you can create wealth. Fear God so that you will prosper all the days of your life (Genesis 17:1; Joshua 1:3–7; Deuteronomy 28:6; Genesis 18:14; Psalm 128:1).

Allow God to orchestrate your steps since he is the creator of your assignment. Instead of listening to the opinions of others, diligently seek God. When you receive the answer, apply God's instructions. Be flexible because God may interrupt your plans. Trust God. He knows the perfect route that you should take (Luke 18:1; Jeremiah 29:13; Proverbs 15:22; Philippians 4:19).

You must be determined and focused on God. Without prayer and discipline, the journey to fulfilling your kingdom assignment could easily be derailed. To receive every blessing, follow God carefully. Your willingness to trust God wholeheartedly allows you to experience his strength and power. Kingdom assignments may become challenging, but never leave your assignment because God will never leave you (Joshua 1:5–6; Hebrews 11:1; Mark 5:34; 2 Chronicles 20:20).

Envision and experience all that God has for you. Become an expert at speaking into existence what the Lord has revealed to you. Your request will be granted if you believe in God. With God, the impossible becomes possible because nothing is too hard for him (Matthew 19:26; Jeremiah 33:3; 2 Corinthians 4:18; Matthew 8:10).

Remember to pray day and night. Rejoice always. Proclaim to all the people that the Lord reigns forever. Are your lips sealed? Or are you talking about the things God has done and is doing in your life? Keep in mind that your faith, praise, and obedience will bring glory to God (Exodus 20:3; 1 Chronicles 16:25-31; Exodus 15:2; Psalm 40:9–10).

2
Secrets to Having Faith in God

> *But seek first his kingdom and his righteousness, and all these things will be given to you as well. Therefore do not worry about tomorrow, for tomorrow will worry about itself. Each day has enough trouble of its own.*
>
> —MATTHEW 6:33–34

God First Instead of Our Desires

OFTENTIMES, WE ALLOW THE cares of this world to dominate our thoughts and actions. When this happens, it's impossible for us to submit to God. According to Romans 8:7, when we live a life controlled by our desires instead of God, we become his enemy. In simple terms, our desires will always fight against God because they reject his authority. Therefore, anything that controls our mind other than God will prevent us from focusing on his kingdom. As a result, pleasing the Lord is no longer a priority. That said, our interest in kingdom affairs have diminished. Instead of committing to our God-given purpose, we are preoccupied with fulfilling our own pleasures, such as wealth, power, and prestige. At some point while pursuing our worldly desires, we become disappointed, impatient, and full of shame. When our desires don't align with God's principles, we will never be satisfied. True happiness can only be found when God is first in everything we do! A person who places God above all things will never be disappointed.

Do you have a desire that the Lord hasn't fulfilled? Perhaps you're thinking that it's impossible for the Lord to meet your needs. Consider what Ephesians 3:20 says: "Now unto him that is able to do exceeding abundantly above all that we ask or think, according to the power that worketh in us" (KJV). Having read the Scripture, do you still have questions about the Lord's ability to provide for you? If so, then look at Philippians 4:19. Within this text, Paul says without any hesitation that the Lord has unlimited resources. This means the Lord is capable of meeting all your needs, no matter how big or small. Due to his infinite knowledge, God knows what we need even before we ask. Unfortunately, many of us forget Revelation 22:13, which states that God is Alpha and Omega, the First and the Last, the Beginning and the End. Therefore, as we read this passage, we are reminded that God is in control of all things, past, present, and future. Isaiah 44:6 also confirms that the Lord declares himself to be the First and the Last, which means no other gods exist. Having said this, God alone is worthy of our worship. This is why we must believe in God and allow ourselves to experience a life-changing transformation. Having faith in the Lord will strengthen our relationship with him. Further, embracing this transformation with an open mind is the key to accepting God's plan for our lives. When we do this, it shows that we have complete confidence that the Lord will meet every need. Thus, our lives are filled with abundant provision when we rely on God's guidance.

Furthermore, the Lord has extended an invitation for us to bring our concerns to him every day. Despite what the Lord has said, most of us fail to respond to his invitation in Matthew 11:28-30, which says, "Come to me, all you who are weary and burdened, and I will give you rest. Take my yoke upon you and learn from me, for I am gentle and humble in heart, and you will find rest for your souls. For my yoke is easy and my burden is light." Mark 6:31 also invites believers to join Christ privately in a quiet place to receive rest. While both Scriptures are true, many Christians prefer to worry. Due to their lack of faith, Christians don't expect God to act on their behalf. Their disbelieving mindset supersedes their ability to receive anything from the Lord. A person who is double-minded in their thinking and indecisive about loving God, according to James 1:7-8, is surely unstable in all their ways. Certainly, God won't do anything for a person who doesn't believe that he will do it.

With this in mind, are you having a hard time surrendering your problems to God? Or are you like many Christians whose loyalty is divided between God and the enemy? One moment, Christians have faith in God's infallible word. Shortly thereafter, they have a hard time trusting God or his word. By the way, God isn't separate from his word. He was and is and will remain the One and only Almighty God. John 1:1 says it best: "In the beginning was the Word, and the Word was with God, and the Word was God." Sadly, many Christians are unable to comprehend God's infinite greatness, endless understanding, everlasting love, and indescribable power. Due to their limited thinking and distrust in God, Christians can't comprehend Hebrews 11:6, which says it's impossible to please God without faith.

All Power Belongs to God

Let me pose this question: how do you lack confidence in the all-powerful God, who Jeremiah 1:5 says formed you in your mother's womb? Yet, you put your trust in humanity. Is your faith in a mere man or God, who made the earth and created mankind? For those who place their hope in a man, let's examine several Scriptures. Once we have examined the text, your trust in God will be strengthened. The writer of Psalm 147:4 declares God's greatness by saying that God placed each star in the sky one by one. Our marvelous, all-knowing God then assigned each star a name. The Holy Scripture Genesis 1:1 also proclaims that God created heaven and the earth. Therefore, God existed before anything.

Without hesitation in Job 38:12, the Lord challenges Job, asking if he has ever commanded the morning to rise. Of course, Job hasn't. Having said this, do you know anyone that has the power to give orders to the rising of the day? I surely don't. In fact, the only person who holds such authority over everything is God. That said, when the Lord speaks, everything must obey him.

The Lord's power is once again displayed in Genesis 1:5. The sacred text states that the earth was dark and unrecognizable until God called the light "day" and the night "darkness." As a result, the text confirms that there was evening and there was morning. Psalm 95:5 also explains the wondrous deeds of God by pointing out that the Lord created the dry land and the sea with his own hands. Job 9:4 describes the Lord as having great wisdom and enormous power. Like Job, King Solomon acknowledged that there is no one on the earth or in heaven like God. Solomon even admits that it's impossible for heaven to contain God (1 Kings 8:22–27).

Moreover, to demonstrate further evidence, the Lord's miraculous power is shown in Exodus 14 when he led the Israelites out of Egypt. As the Israelites were leaving Egypt, Pharaoh and his army relentlessly pursued them. In spite of this, God intervened when the Israelites approached the Red Sea. The Lord then separated the waters and created a path for the Israelites to cross over on dry land. Once the Israelites crossed the water safely, God caused Pharaoh and his army to drown at sea. On that day, the Israelites witnessed the mighty hand of God fighting for them. After this miracle, the Israelites feared the Lord and put their trust in him. The Israelite experience reveals God's protection, faithfulness, and his unwavering love for his people. That being said, the Lord's power is yet again shown amongst the Israelites. His power is never-ending, and he rules forever and ever. In fact, Daniel 2:44 makes a bold true statement, saying the Lord's kingdom will never end!

Once again, I will ask the question, how can anyone doubt the magnificent power of God? His power is limitless, incomparable, and undeniable. Even David said in Psalm 145:3 that there is no way to fully grasp God's greatness because it surpasses all human comprehension. Consider this: a lack of confidence in the true and living God will cause us to waver in our faith. The more we rely on ourselves, the less faith we have in God's power. Eventually we will develop stress and anxiety once we are aware of our human limitations. Think about this: Ecclesiastes 1:2 says if we aren't living life with God, then life is meaningless. Therefore, to survive in a chaotic world, guidance from God is necessary. Sooner or later, we must accept what Psalm 62:11 says: "God has spoken once, Twice I have heard this: That power *belongs* to God" (NKJV). The apostle Paul also recognizes God's supreme authority in Colossians 1:16-17, which means that there is no end to God's power and control in the universe. Therefore, because God is in control of all creation, he has the power to change and rearrange anything he desires. Because of the Lord's vast love, Acts 17:27 states, the Lord is never far from any of us. Proverbs 15:3 explains that the eyes of the Lord are everywhere. Better yet, the Lord is omnipresent, which means that he is always available when we need him. The Lord can simultaneously help you and me while ministering to others. This shows the depths of his love for each of us individually. Bearing this in mind, his love knows no boundaries. His grace is abundant; therefore, let us seek his counsel everyday.

Furthermore, every situation that you encounter will change when you turn to God. However, John 3:30 points out, you will not see change if God doesn't become more important while you become less important. Is the Lord everything to you? Knowing Christ as our Lord is one of the most important things we learn from our Bible. By reading our Bible, we can gain a better understanding of Jesus's character, his teachings, and his love for us. In addition, we will learn how to serve him and follow his example.

Further, a proclamation is announced by God in Exodus 3:14, which says, God's name is "I am!" When God urged Moses to deliver the Israelites out of Egypt, Moses said to God, "When the Israelites ask me your name, what should I say?" The Almighty God said: "Tell the Israelites that my name is 'I am!' The God of your ancestors." Has the Lord said to you, "I am the Lord your God?" Do you accept him as your Lord? If so, are you living your life differently after accepting Christ as your Lord? Accepting Christ as our Lord gives us confidence that we don't have to rely on anything or anyone for assistance. Why? Because the Lord is self-sufficient, and he doesn't need anyone's help. He is the creator of life, and there is only one Lord. Without God, we are nothing, and apart from him, nothing was created that has been created, according to John 1:3. Now then, we can stay focused and motivated, knowing that the Lord is our healer, provider, counselor, and whatever else we need him to be. Wouldn't you agree?

Faith in God and Provision is Guaranteed

Lastly, Hebrews 13:8 boldly affirms, "Jesus Christ is the same yesterday and today and forever." Therefore, after reading this passage, it is evident that Christ will always be faithful to us. Psalm 100:5 also proves that God's unconditional love and faithfulness will continue forever to all generations. The Lord is trustworthy, full of love, holy, and simply amazing. Knowing this, we should always have a desire to praise his holy name. With an attitude of gratefulness, we can confess what David said in Psalm 34:1: "I will bless the Lord at all times: his praise shall continually be in my mouth" (KJV). Regardless of our circumstances and even when things don't look good, we must remain confident in our Father, El Shaddai, God Almighty!

Moreover, when we trust God, we can do as Christ says in Matthew 6:34: stop worrying about our lives, especially since tomorrow isn't promised to any of us. Keeping the words of Christ at the forefront of our mind, we must get in the habit of enjoying today because tomorrow has its own challenges. Of course, if you haven't developed a habit of praying consistently, then worrying is inevitable. Unfortunately, we tend to wrestle with the spirit of worry. Worrying about our problems will prevent us from seeking God's wisdom. Essentially, when we worry, we are telling the Lord that our problems are beyond his ability to solve.

On the other hand, by asking the Lord for help, we acknowledge the importance of his advice and guidance. As we accept the Lord's assistance, we can be certain that our anxieties will be replaced with faith, peace, love, and joy. Relying on God also demonstrates that you are intentional about your desire to know, trust, and serve him. Above all, your intentional worship of the Lord reveals that you are more interested in having a kingdom perspective instead of a secular mindset. God's wisdom is available to you because of your deliberate worship, for it is written in Psalm 23:1 that you will not lack anything because God is first in your life. From this day forward, the Lord's provisions are guaranteed to you. Because you trust God, there are no restrictions on your blessings. You have God's favor, honor, and riches. Therefore, continue to be clothed with a kingdom mindset, having the confidence to walk in the authority given to you by Christ.

The Centurion's Sick Servant

That is why I did not even consider myself worthy to come to you. But say the word, and my servant will be healed.

—LUKE 7:7

Luke, a doctor and a Gentile Christian, begins chapter 7 of his Gospel by explaining to his readers, with faith and expectation, that Jesus Christ, the miracle worker, can do the impossible. Luke proves his point by presenting to his audience the story of a man who needed a miracle because he was about to die. The sick man had a master, a Gentile Roman centurion who was very concerned about his servant's health. Has a situation in your life left you feeling incapacitated? Do you blame yourself for your condition or someone else? Better yet, has your condition prevented you from obeying God? Think on this: when our circumstances become unbearable, it's impossible to share the gospel to a dying world. Due to the excruciating pain, we are unable to trust God. Unfortunately, the distraction of the pain and feeling powerless will cause us to ignore God's gentle voice. Disregarding the Lord's soft voice implies that we don't believe he has the power to rescue us. Instead of focusing on the pain, we must concentrate on God's invitation to rest in his arms. When we accept God's offer, which is a place of peaceful rest, we are no longer worried because our mind is refreshed and our soul is filled with joy. Once our faith is renewed, the Lord can perform the inconceivable, or even better, a miracle.

Prior to becoming sick, the servant was a dedicated worker. The centurion, his master, loved his servant dearly. Out of love for his servant, the centurion sent the Jewish elders to speak with Jesus. He wanted the elders to ask Jesus to heal his sick servant. The centurion had heard about Jesus performing many healing miracles. Despite never meeting Jesus, the centurion believed that his beloved servant would be healed. The centurion's humility and great reverence for the almighty God is obvious in Luke 7:7, when he says, "I am not even worthy to come and meet you. Just say the word from where you are, and my servant will be healed" (NLT). What about you? Do you feel unworthy of being in God's presence? Are you dealing with hopelessness, shame, or guilt? If so, please understand that the Lord heals the wounds of the brokenhearted, according to Psalm 147:3. Therefore, the Lord is never far from any of us. God will hear us whenever we are ready to talk to him. He is a caretaker, healer, and a protector who will revive our troubled souls. That said, the Lord's incredible love for us is confirmed in Isaiah 46:4, which states that will he care for us all the days of our lives. This means the Lord will never get tired of us, no matter how old we are. In fact, the Lord's love, mercy, and gentle care for us will extend far beyond our parents.

Consider this: as we approach a holy God, we are conscious of our sin. In light of this, we know that we are unworthy of being near God. However, because of the Lord's forgiving heart and endless love, we can always run to his safe and loving arms. Now then, we will remain hopeful about God because he knows how it feels to be a human. It was John the Baptist who testified that Jesus, the Son of God, was in the world. He continues by saying in John 1:14 that the Word (Christ) became flesh and lived among us.

Jesus Christ was both fully man and fully God. Although he was tempted in every way, Hebrews 4:15 declares that the Son of God did not sin. Having read what John has said about Christ, you can be confident that the Son of God understands your weaknesses and strengths. Therefore, keep pressing until you can quietly rest in the Lord's safe and caring arms.

Beautifully Made by God

Furthermore, we are told in Genesis 1:27 that God created all of us to be like him. Yes, you were created in God's image. With this in mind, your Father is pleased with how he made you! Perhaps you don't believe how precious you are to God. Just in case this is your story, Isaiah 49:16 says the Lord has written your name on the palms of his hands. Having said this, the Lord is always thinking about you. Therefore, it's impossible for the Lord to forget about you. Why? Because the Lord sees your name when he opens his hands. As you think about the previous Scripture, God your Father will always love you, treasure you, and protect you. For this reason, you must remember that you are valuable to God. Keeping this in mind, stop allowing people to determine your worth. Better yet, the approval of others isn't necessary. Now is the time to look to God, the creator of everything. With his gentle hands, Psalm 139:14 proclaims that you are beautiful and unique, fearfully and amazingly made by God. Need I say more? You are perfect and important to God!

As a matter of fact, God has given you more power than you could ever imagine. The Bible clearly says in 2 Timothy 1:7 that you don't have the Spirit of fear, but you are fearless and powerful. However, it is essential that you learn how to use God's power for his purposes only. Establishing a meaningful relationship with God is the key to utilizing his power. Believe it or not, you were created to have a relationship with Christ! Yes, God loves you and wants to spend eternity with you. The apostle Paul explains in Romans 5:8, that Christ loved us so much that he died for us while we were still sinners. Therefore, if you haven't accepted the free gift of salvation from Christ, the time is now. Jesus says in John 6:37 that whoever the Father gives him will never be rejected. The Lord is waiting to commune with you. Don't delay—seek the Lord today!

The Power of Intercession

Moreover, the Roman officer demonstrated his belief in the power of intercession by sending the Jewish elders to meet with Jesus. There was no doubt in the centurion's mind that the elders could pray and receive answers from God. Luke 7:4 describes how persistent the elders were when they met Jesus. For example, as soon as the elders saw Jesus, they begged him to go to the centurion's house and heal the servant. While petitioning Jesus to heal the sick servant, the elders also said great things about the centurion. The elders then praised the centurion for building the synagogue. They also commended the centurion for loving his country and his people. After speaking very highly of the centurion, the elders asked Jesus to grant their request. Jesus was deeply moved by the remarkable words spoken by the elders. As a result, Jesus agreed to visit the centurion's home. Do you have a relationship with your pastor or the elders of your church? How often do you ask the church leaders to intercede on your behalf? Better yet, do you have friends or family members that will pray with you? Even if you don't have anyone to pray with you, the Lord has given you the authority to pray for yourself and others.

On the other hand, when we don't know what to pray, Romans 8:26 reassures us by saying that the Lord will intercede for us. This means that you don't have to worry about your problems or those you are praying for. You must always remember that you are an heir to Christ. You have a helper, namely the Holy Spirit, who knows what you need before you ask. That said, continue to make your request known to God. By doing this, you will experience God's peace in every situation. Think about this: Philippians 4:7 says that God's peace will control our feelings and thoughts when we allow him to reign in our hearts. Now then, as you pray for others, the Lord's peace will also be given to them.

The Centurion's Faith Moves Christ

As Jesus is approaching the centurion's home, Luke 7:6 says the friends of the centurion met him. The centurion told his friends to tell Jesus, "Lord, you don't have to come to my house." The centurion understood that Christ didn't have to be in his home to heal his servant. His trust and extraordinary confidence are evident when he said to Christ, "Speak a word of healing and my servant will be healed." Are you a person of faith who believes that whatever the Lord says, it shall happen? Maybe your faith isn't on that level yet. When we trust God's plan, it demonstrates an act of faith. Even if you have little faith, you can open your mouth right now and ask God to increase your faith. A person whose faith is like the centurion will believe every spoken word from the lips of God. Therefore, having this type of faith shows that you expect results when Christ speaks.

Lastly, Luke 7:9 says Jesus turned to his followers after hearing the unwavering faith of the centurion. Jesus then publicly announced that no one in Israel exemplified faith like the centurion leader. At that point, the centurion's friends returned to the house and saw the sick servant's health restored. As a believer, what kind of faith are you displaying to people around you? The Roman officer's story reveals that we must believe in the power of God if we are expecting something phenomenal to happen. With this in mind, you must get rid of your doubting mindset because only your faith will please the Lord. To believe in the power of God we must frequently fill our mind with the Holy Scriptures. When we saturate our mind with God's word, our faith is strengthened. As God's word transforms our thinking, we will no longer question his authority. At times, having faith in God may seem foolish or strange, but trusting God will bring great blessings. Sometimes, God's promises will not happen immediately. Yet, if you are patient, the Lord will be amazed at your persistent, courageous faith. Having said that, the Lord's blessings will surpass your expectations.

Power Points on Having Faith in God

The vision that God has given you will require faith, commitment, endurance, and diligence. However, the vision will only come to pass once you have faith in the unseen. In other words, you must trust what God has said to you. His word is your evidence that the vision will take place. Do you have the audacity to accept God's word as truth? If so, remain focused; the Lord is with you. Because of God's great power, you have tenacity, wisdom, and resilience to accomplish anything. Listed below are five Power Points called F.A.I.T.H., which will help you receive what God has for you.

F aith in God can only be attained if you spend time with him. You will develop a stronger relationship with God when you pray and study your Bible. By doing this, you will learn how to rely on God. He is trustworthy and will supply all your needs (Romans 10:17; Proverbs 3:5-6; Psalm 37:3-6; Acts 20:21-24; Psalms 25:1; 40:4; Romans 8:24).

A sk God first because you are inexperienced. You may think you understand the path, but only the Lord knows the way. The Lord will illuminate your path so that you can complete your assignment successfully. Trust the Lord. He will honor his word. The Lord is good to those who have faith in him (1 Kings 3:9; 2 Chronicles 1:10; James 1:5; Proverbs 16:9; Jeremiah 10:23).

I nstructions are given when you seek the Lord's advice. Stay committed to God and you will not be led astray by anyone or your emotions. Following the Lord's plans for your life brings success (Psalm 16:7-8; Proverbs 4:7; 16:3; Psalm 119:105).

T esting your faith is something that God will do from time to time. Challenges are part of your assignment. God is watching, so be careful how you react. Are you persistent or will you throw in the towel when times get hard? Don't be afraid to talk to God. He is waiting to hear from you. Asking God questions is not a sign of lack of trust in him. Keep going and finish your assignment; don't quit (2 Corinthians 4:18; James 1:7-8; Exodus 15:13; 1 Kings 8:57; Romans 8:31; Ephesians 6:10).

Holy Scripture can teach you how to be wiser than anyone you know. But you must have faith in God's word. Your life will be transformed once you fall in love with the Bible. Reading the Bible regularly will help you remember God's promises and his commandments (Psalms 40:8; 119:97-104; Job 1:8; Proverbs 4:13; 9:12).

3

Secrets to Knowing God's Purpose for Your Life

Going a little farther, he fell with his face to the ground and prayed, "My Father, if it is possible, may this cup be taken from me. Yet not as I will, but as you will."

—MATTHEW 26:39

Jesus Christ Is Lord

THE PLAN OF GOD begins to unfold in Matthew 26:65 when the high priest accused Jesus of Blasphemy. Blasphemy is the act of professing to be God. Anyone that commits blasphemy, according to Leviticus 24:16, shall be put to death. However, Mark 14:62 records that when the high priest asked Christ if he was the Son of God, his response was, "I am." Christ under no circumstances hesitated about affirming his kingdom when questioned by the high priest. Unafraid and unashamed, Christ knew he would be executed when he declared himself as the Messiah. The chief priests wanted Christ dead because in their eyes, he was making himself equal to God.

Unfortunately, the chief priests refused to accept Christ's authority because of their insecurities. Christ was viewed as a threat by the Jewish leaders despite their influence within their own community. The high priest was an important figure within the Israelite community. Throughout history, the highest religious authority was held by the high priest. The high priest was responsible for overseeing various religious rituals and affairs. However, as the popularity of Christ grew among the people, the Jewish leaders became intimidated, envious, and full of resentment. Nonetheless, Christ wasn't bothered by their lack of confidence in him. In fact, Christ challenged his opponents because of their impure motives. Although the religious leaders taught the law, they didn't live according to Scripture. As the high priests, their job was to lead the people closer to God. Instead, they were more focused on receiving recognition and honor. As noted in Mark 12:38–40, the Jewish leaders were more concerned about outward appearances than their relationship with God. For example, the leaders often wore Scriptures on their foreheads. They would also pray long prayers in public so that people would notice them. Even though the leaders were committed to teaching God's word, their stubborn hearts and hypocritical ways prevented them from truly worshiping God.

The Ministry of Christ

Furthermore, Christ was the ultimate example of servanthood. His ministry, though short, impacted many lives due to his love for people. While proclaiming the gospel, Christ performed many miracles. Christ miraculously healed many people although they were afflicted with incurable diseases. Luke 7:21–22 states that Christ restored eyesight to the blind, raised the dead, healed many who suffered from chronic diseases, empowered the lame to walk, and cleansed individuals possessed by unclean spirits. Yet, the mission of Christ was to give his life as a ransom for a dying world. Even though Christ committed no acts of violence, the Savior of the world was punished for our sins. Because of his love for you and me, Matthew 27:28-35 says Jesus Christ was tortured, humiliated, and then hung on a cross. That said, his incomprehensible love for the world has made it possible for all of us to have eternal life, according to John 3:16.

Moreover, John 3:3 specifically says that no one can experience the kingdom of God unless they are spiritually reborn. This act of spiritual rebirth can only be achieved by having faith in God. Faith in God is the key to receiving an everlasting life. With this in mind, are you ready to make Christ Lord over your life? If Christ isn't your Lord, then now is the time to commit to him. Would you like to know how easy it is to say yes to the Lord? If so, Paul makes this very clear in Romans 10:9 by saying, "If you declare with your mouth, 'Jesus is Lord,' and believe in your heart that God raised him from the dead, you will be saved." Because of your heartfelt declaration of faith, this demonstrates that you acknowledge Jesus as Lord over your life. By recognizing him as the Son of God, your past, present, and future sins are forgiven. Why? Because the Lord paid the price at the cross for your sins. Romans 8:1 also explains that there is no condemnation for those who love Jesus Christ. Bearing this in mind, the gospel's number-one priority is not to condemn but to save. Not only does the gospel offer God's great love but we are given the opportunity to experience his grace and forgiveness. From this day forward, Romans 5:1 has confirmed you as righteous because of your confession and faith in God. Now that you have a personal relationship with God, you will experience his love, grace, and guidance. As you continue your journey, the Lord will help you live a life that honors him.

Christ's Assignment

Of course, Jesus Christ the gentle servant didn't have to bear the iniquities of all humanity. In fact, Matthew 26:39 says Christ asked his Father to release him from his divine assignment before he was arrested by his enemies. Have you asked the Lord to release you from your assignment? Reflect on this: you didn't choose your assignment—the Lord did. With this in mind, you can be certain that God is confident that you can perform the job. However, you must be careful that your emotions do not interfere with your ability to complete your assignment. The Lord is depending on you; therefore, you must fulfill the assignment. By the way, having faith in God is the only way to accomplish this great task. Along with trusting God, you will have to believe in the vision to carry it out. In the event that you lack courage or your vision is dim, ask God for help. After receiving a sharper vision, a little bit of faith, and God's guidance, you will accomplish your assignment.

Despite receiving clear instructions from his Father, Christ still struggled to fulfill his assignment. For example, Matthew 26:39 describes how Christ fell on his face and prayed, "My Father, if it is possible, may this cup be taken from me. Yet not as I will, but as you will." Feeling overwhelmed and saddened in the depths of his soul, Christ prayed to his Father three times about his assignment before fulfilling it. The agony that Christ felt came about because, as a man who committed no sin, he began to feel the pain caused by the sins of the world. Whenever there is sin, pain is always involved. The results of sin aren't felt immediately, but suffering will eventually come. Unfortunately, the impact of a person's sin will affect many generations after the crime is committed. The moment we understand the effects of sin, we must obey the Lord's commandment. Exodus 20:3 boldly proclaims no one or anything should come before God. The Lord will not share his glory with anyone, including you.

Commit to Christ

That being said, the message of Matthew 6:24 is clear: we cannot serve God and the things of the world. Hence, we are separated from God when we choose to ignore his commandments and sin. Having said this, the Lord becomes jealous when he isn't first. When the Lord isn't a priority, Psalm 79:5 declares that the Lord's jealousy is like a burning fire, destroying everything in its path. In other words, the Lord will not tolerate our worship for anyone or anything but him. Consider what Revelation 3:16 says: the Lord will reject us if we are indecisive about serving him. Taking this into account, when we serve both the enemy and God, we are called lukewarm Christians. This type of behavior is unacceptable; therefore, because of our sin, punishment is inescapable. Not only are we punished, but the Lord will punish the children for the sins that the parents commit, as stated in Exodus 20:5.

This is why we are also told in Psalm 79:8–9 to immediately ask the Lord to forgive the sins of our ancestors so that we are not penalized for their ungodly behavior. Ultimately, sin leads to death because of the power that sin has over a person's life. Paul reminds the saints in Romans 6:23 that the wages of sin are death and yet the gift of God is eternal life in Jesus Christ. Therefore, when you commit to an eternal life with the Lord, sin does not control your life—Christ does. When the Lord controls your life, you have been set free from a sinful lifestyle to a life of holiness. Now that you have been delivered from the bondage of sin, aren't you glad? Having said that, as described in Colossians 1:22, Christ sees you as holy. That's right, the Lord has erased the sins that you have committed. Psalm 103:12 also confirms that as far as the east is from the west, the Lord has removed our sins from us. Since this is true, you can ask God to give you the desire to live a life that is pleasing to him. Cultivating an authentic and meaningful relationship with the Lord should include prayer, fasting, and reading your Bible. While you are implementing these spiritual tools, you will surely increase your knowledge of God. When we learn about God, this will definitely please him.

Prayer Gives Us Access to God

Further, once you meditate on God's word, you will notice that God is eager to have consistent dialogue with you. Do you believe that the Lord enjoys hearing your voice? Hopefully you do, but if not, take a moment and read Jeremiah 29:12. This Scripture is inspiring because a gracious invitation has been extended to us to talk with God. In view of this, we can be assured that God will listen and answer since he has requested our presence. Isn't this great news? For every unanswered or perplexing question, the Lord says he will answer you! As you embrace this great news, keep this in mind: whatever you're facing, the solution is to turn to God and not everyone else.

With that said, prayer is a powerful weapon that Christians have at their disposal. However, you must pray consistently if you expect the Lord to respond to your prayers. Spending time with the Lord is the key to receiving an answer from God. These special moments in prayer with God will also create an atmosphere of intimacy. Whenever there is intimacy, you will have direct access to the throne room of heaven. Therefore, Hebrews 4:16 tells us to approach God with confidence and discover his grace to assist us when we need it. Now then, consider this: as you spend time with God, you will learn how to pray his will instead of your own. Because you have prayed the Father's will, John 15:7 says that whatever you ask, you will receive.

Spiritual Relationships Bring Us Closer to God

Furthermore, Christ provides an example of how to handle difficult assignments. For instance, Matthew 26:39–42 states that instead of talking to the disciples about fulfilling his assignment, Christ spoke to his Father. Before going to the cross, Christ knew the type of death sentence he would face. It was also evident to Christ that the disciples weren't mature enough to handle what he was about to encounter. The disciples didn't have the capacity to give Christ wise counsel. Are you involved in relationships that hinder your spiritual growth? Developing meaningful relationships is vital to nurturing your relationship with Christ. Therefore, you must be cautious of who you connect and converse with. Those closest to you will have a tremendous impact on your beliefs, values, and actions. Whether positive or negative, people in your circle will always influence you. This is why it is necessary to examine your relationships to ensure they are in line with your faith. Your spiritual relationships should lead to greater intimacy with God, not distance you from him. Any relationships that separate you from the Lord is a problem. Essentially, your spiritual relationships should help you gain a deeper understanding of God. What's the purpose of having spiritual connections if they aren't improving your relationship with Christ? Think about this: Proverbs 27:17 specifically says like-minded people improve the minds of each other. When two spiritually minded friends come together, they provide insight and clarity about spiritually related ideas. As they develop in God's wisdom, like-minded individuals also challenge each other by living a righteous lifestyle. With God's wisdom, people that think alike see things from God's perspective. Brilliant ideas are also formed when two spiritually minded people come together.

Humility and Fulfilling Your Assignment

Meanwhile, as Christ prayed to the Father about his assignment, Luke 22:42-44 explains that his prayers became so intense, the sweat dripping from his face looked like drops of blood when it fell to the ground. At that moment, the Father, having compassion for his Son Jesus, sent an angel from heaven to strengthen and motivate him. The support from his Father encouraged Christ to continue his mission for the kingdom. Christ humbled himself and accepted the assignment by saying to the Father, "I seek to please you; therefore, not my will, but let your will be done in my life." Jesus's deep personal commitment to do the will of his Father exemplifies his trust in God's plans. Like Jesus, you may find your assignment impossible to accomplish. However, the above sentence illustrates that following Christ's example of humility is necessary to fulfill your assignment. Consider what Proverbs 22:4 says: a person who practices humility fears God. Therefore, when the spirit of humility is pursued, the Lord will provide riches, honor, and a long-lasting life.

Without humility, we will develop arrogant and prideful tendencies. Humility is a vital ingredient for building and maintaining healthy relationships. It is only through humility that imperfect people can learn and grow from one another. Also, by embracing humility, we are recognizing the need for guidance from God. With this in mind, our worship for the Lord will be enriched when we humble ourselves under his leadership. To worship God, one must have a spirit of unselfishness. Thus, keeping God first in your life says you are determined to do his will. You also understand and accept that God's way is the best way for your life. As a result of having an unwavering attitude, the Lord will give you strategies to complete your assignment. He will also empower you with confidence, zeal, and passion because of your Christ-centered mentality. The Lord will help you remain steadfast and unstoppable in fulfilling your kingdom assignment.

Mordecai Pursuing His Purpose on Foreign Territory

> *For if you remain silent at this time, relief and deliverance for the Jews will arise from another place, but you and your father's family will perish. And who knows but that you have come to your royal position for such a time as this?*
>
> —*Esther 4:14*

After the death of King Nebuchadnezzar, the Medes and the Persians joined forces and conquered the Babylonian Empire, according to Daniel 5:30. This bond between the two nations created the rise of the Medo-Persian Empire. The Medo-Persian Empire was known as one of the most powerful and wealthiest nations in the world. During this time, the kings of Persia played a significant role in Jewish affairs. For example, the Jews were exiled for seventy years from their native land and taken to Babylon. After seventy years of captivity, Ezra 1:1–3 records Cyrus, king of Persia, was chosen by God to free the Jews and return them to their homeland, Jerusalem.

Many years later after the release of the Jews, Esther 2:5 says a God-fearing man by the name of Mordecai lived in Susa, the capital of Persia, during the reign of King Xerxes. Mordecai loved his brethren and Jerusalem, but he knew that his divine purpose was connected to the Persian Empire. What about you? Do you feel that your purpose in life is connected to something greater than you could envision? How would the idea of fulfilling your purpose influence the way you make decisions in your life? Has the Lord spoken to you about completing your purpose? When God speaks, we must listen carefully and respond appropriately. The road to achieving our God-given purpose is often paved with obstacles. Have you encountered any setbacks while fulfilling your assignment? If so, what strategies did you use to stay motivated in pursuing your purpose? Or have you completely disobeyed God and didn't do your assignment? Consider this: before you were born, God perfectly designed a unique assignment just for you. Now that you know this, when you fail to follow God's instructions, you are disobeying him.

This may surprise you; many people encounter stumbling blocks while trying to fulfill their purpose. In many instances, it's hard to stay focused while working on what God has called us to do. Unfortunately, we become discouraged when the assignment becomes challenging. This happens because we lack confidence in our Father, God. Without faith in God, we will neglect our kingdom assignment. The best advice is to consult God the creator of the assignment, the one who has all the answers. As believers, we must have faith in God's ability. Having faith in God, along with determination, we can overcome any obstacles that come our way. We must also remember: every roadblock is an opportunity for us to learn and grow.

Therefore, when we are confident in God's power, we won't hesitate to ask him for assistance. Do you ask God for help? If not, why haven't you? The Lord will never get tired of helping you. Have you read Isaiah 40:28? Just in case you haven't, the passage says that the Lord who created the universe is never exhausted but always ready to assist those in need. Consider what David says in

Psalm 16:7: "I will praise the LORD, who counsels me; even at night my heart instructs me." Within this chapter, David is expressing his gratitude toward the Lord. Whatever David faced, he knew the Lord would be right by his side. Unlike man, who has human limitations, the Lord listens to the needs of his children. The Lord takes pleasure in providing encouragement, guidance, and support to his children. Having said this, Proverbs 8:14 is another excellent Scripture that encourages believers to seek the Lord's counsel. Keeping this in mind, we will indeed receive an answer when we set aside time to communicate with the Lord. With God's advice, we can make an intelligent decision concerning the issue. Besides, we are honoring God when we allow him to handle our situations his way. With this in mind, we must stay connected and committed to God to accomplish our kingdom assignment.

After reading Psalm 37:23, I am convinced that when we trust God to direct our steps, surely our path is blessed. I believe Mordecai also understood this Scripture. Mordecai's willingness to trust God in a foreign land gave him the opportunity to embrace a life full of purpose. While under the Persian leadership of King Xerxes, Mordecai was very successful. Although he faced many trials, including death, he never rejected the Lord or his kingdom assignment. Mordecai's strong and fearless spirit can be traced back to the tribe of Benjamin. According to Esther 2:5, Mordecai was a Benjaminite. He was also a descendant of Kish. Kish had been carried from Jerusalem into captivity by King Nebuchadnezzar of Babylon. This same man Kish was also the father of Saul, Israel's first king, according to 1 Samuel 9:2.

Esther Prepares for Her Purpose

Mordecai also had a younger cousin named Hadassah. As noted in Esther 2:7, Mordecai adopted Hadassah after her parents died. Hadassah, also known as Esther, was one of the young virgins chosen when King Xerxes of Persia replaced his wife, Queen Vashti. According to Esther 2:4, the king issued a decree for a new queen. Many of the young women throughout the Persian

Empire, including Esther, were brought to the king's palace. Once the young women arrived at the palace, they were placed under the care of the king's eunuch, Hegai. Hegai was responsible for making sure the women completed a twelve-month beauty program. After completing the program, the women met King Xerxes. The beauty regimen included very expensive fragrance, oil of myrrh, and cosmetics. For the first six months, the women were endowed with special perfumes and beauty products. The remaining six months, the women received massages with oil of myrrh. The oil of myrrh was used to moisturize the women's skin, making them feel soft, smooth, and beautiful.

As stated in Genesis 43:11, myrrh was also given as a gift by Israel to his son, Joseph. Within this text, Israel emphasized that myrrh was one of the best products in the land. The ancient Near Eastern culture considered myrrh an expensive and acceptable gift. In Exodus 30:23–30, liquid myrrh was listed as one of the ingredients used to consecrate the priest, the tabernacle, and its furnishings. Liquid myrrh and other special ingredients were declared by the Lord as a sacred anointing oil. Moses was instructed by the Lord to anoint the priests with the special holy oil. It is also written in Exodus 30:32 that God commanded Moses and the Israelites against imitating the holy anointing oil. In addition, the king had to be anointed with the holy oil before serving as Israel's king. Once anointed with the oil, the king vowed to pray and follow God's counsel. Have you struggled with following God's advice? When we follow God, we are given extraordinary strength. After being anointed with the sacred oil, the king of Israel was endowed with power. For instance, 1 Samuel 16:13 says that David received divine power to do the Lord's will after Samuel anointed him with the sacred oil. Further, John 19:40 also points out that before Jesus was laid in the tomb, Nicodemus and Joseph wrapped Jesus's body with a linen cloth, along with liquid myrrh and aloe. Myrrh was also given to help reduce the pain when a person was about to die. While on the cross, Mark 15:23 mentions that this is the same myrrh, which was mixed with wine and offered to Jesus, but he refused to drink it.

Now that I have told you about the importance of myrrh, let's return to the story of Esther. When Esther entered the royal palace, her pleasant demeanor and eye-catching beauty caught the attention of everyone in King Xerxes's empire. From the moment Hegai the eunuch set eyes on Esther, she became his favorite virgin. Without hesitation, Hegai made sure that Esther received her beauty treatments, along with her special food. Esther was also given seven young women to assist her. Esther 2:9 also says that Hegai went as far as making sure that Esther and her servants lived in the most luxurious part of the harem.

Finally, after being pampered for a year, the women had a chance to meet the king. Amazed at Esther's beauty, King Xerxes quickly fell in love with her. Esther 2:17 states that the king immediately made Esther the queen of Persia. As described in the previous paragraph, the virgins of Persia prepared for one year to spend time with a mere man. How often do you prepare to meet your King, Jesus Christ? Do you have a desire to be in God's presence? If not, you should! Psalm 105:4 proclaims that believers should always seek the presence of the Lord. We are also told in Psalm 37:4 to consistently make every effort to please the Lord. An excellent example of pleasing the Lord is to do his will. On the other hand, if God isn't viewed as a necessity in your life, then it is unlikely that you will pursue him. Our deliberate pursuit of God's presence is one of the greatest acts of worship. By pursuing God intentionally, we are demonstrating that we cannot live without him. This type of relationship establishes a deeper intimacy with God. Spending precious moments with the Lord will teach us how to fully surrender to him. Having intimacy with the Lord brings fulfillment and satisfaction in our lives.

As a result of the Lord's endless and abundant love and tender mercy toward us, our praise for him should never end. With a grateful heart, Psalm 105:1 says we should publicly announce God's greatness by telling everyone what he has done for us. Finally, since God is the creator of the universe, we must do as Psalm 150:6 boldly says: "Let everything that has breath praise the Lord." Therefore, anything that has breath should purposefully pursue and praise God.

Mordecai's Promotion

Meanwhile, Esther 2:19 says Mordecai was promoted by King Xerxes to serve in the royal palace. The king also elevated a man name Haman to the second-most-powerful position in his empire. Haman was a descendant of the Amalekites. Genesis 36:16 says the Amalekites were descendants of Esau. Esau, according to Genesis 25:24–26, is the brother of Jacob. Jacob is also known as Israel. Esau was the eldest son of Isaac and Rebekah. As the firstborn son, if Esau's father were deceased, Esau would automatically become the head of his family. Although Esau was the eldest son, he showed little interest in receiving his inheritance. In exchange for a cup of soup, Esau relinquished his birthright to his brother. One day, when Jacob was cooking soup, his brother Esau asked for a cup of soup. Seeing that his brother was very hungry, Jacob decided to take advantage of the situation. According to Genesis 25:31, Jacob said to Esau that he would give him a cup of soup on one condition: "Sell me your birthright." Instead of denying his hunger pains, Genesis 25:33 explains that Esau surrendered to Jacob's demands. Unfortunately, Esau's decision to give up his birthright was based on immediate gratification. Even more unfortunate, Esau did not consider the consequences of his reckless decision.

With this in mind, there is great danger ahead when we make decisions based on impulse. While Jacob may have taken advantage of Esau, Genesis 25:32 says that Esau said to his brother, "What good is the birthright to me?" Sadly, Esau detested his birthright and hated his brother Jacob. In Genesis 27:41, Esau made a vow to murder his brother after his father died. Esau's hatred and hostility for Jacob was passed down through his bloodline to his grandson, Amalek. Genesis 36:12 records that this is the same Amalek who became the founder of the Amalekite tribe. Thus, the war between Jacob (Israel) and Esau's descendants continued for centuries.

In fact, Exodus 17:8 says the first attack from the Amalekites took place when the Israelites left Egypt while on their way to the promised land. The Israelites were at their weakest moment and exhausted when the Amalekites, having no fear of God, viciously attacked them. The Amalekites saw that the women, children, and the sick could not keep up with the rest of the Israelites, so they assaulted them. This type of behavior was cruel and dishonest. The attack on the Israelites made the Lord very angry. The Lord despises anyone who deals with his children in this manner. If anyone intentionally causes any harm to God's children, they will feel his wrath. Having said this, retaliation isn't necessary; Romans 12:19 provides great counsel, saying that vengeance belongs to God. Therefore, we must step back from the situation and let the Lord punish our offenders. Deuteronomy 25:19 also describes how the Lord cursed the Amalekites by commanding the Israelites to remove the tribe from the face of the earth. Since the Amalekites dealt with God's people in such a ruthless manner, the Lord's judgment toward them would be the same. This meant that the Israelites would have to exterminate every beast, child, and adult, according to 1 Samuel 15:3. Unfortunately, not all the Amalekites were killed. Had the army of Israel destroyed the tribe like the Lord instructed, no one would have remembered the Amalekites' existence.

Moreover, when Haman, a descendant of the Amalekites, came face-to-face with the Jew Mordecai, history repeated itself. Haman also had the same hateful spirit as his ancestors. As the highest-ranking officer in Persia, the king's servants were commanded to bow down to Haman. After hearing the king's decree, the royal staff knelt and worshiped Haman. Nevertheless, Esther 3:2 says Mordecai rejected the king's decree. Mordecai wasn't being malicious or arrogant toward the Persian king. The man of God was simply fulfilling God's purpose by staying true to the commandments of his religion. In other words, Mordecai's loyalty was to God and not a man.

As believers, we too must decide if we are going to be faithful in serving Christ. Without a solid commitment to God, at some point, we will become unfaithful to him. The Lord isn't pleased when we refuse to commit our life to him. Exodus 20:3–5 says God is against his children worshiping anyone other than him. As described in Psalm 16:4, pain and suffering will multiply for anyone who pursues other gods. Therefore, any time we revere anyone other than God, it is called idolatry. Think about this: the Lord is pleased when we fully submit ourselves to him. The Lord isn't looking for a part-time love affair with us. How would you feel if someone loved you part-time? Better yet, what if the Lord only loved you part-time? I'm sure you wouldn't like it, and neither does the Lord. Proverbs 15:9 is clear on what the Lord takes delight in, and that is a person who pursues righteousness. Exodus 20:5 also confirms that the Lord is indeed a jealous God. In view of this, the Lord has no tolerance for our powerless idols that we worship. By contrast, in Psalm 147:11, the Lord takes pleasure in those who worship and trust him.

Opposition Is Common While Pursuing Your Purpose

Furthermore, it is reported in Esther 3:2 that Mordecai's colleagues accused him of violating the king's decree because he refused to bow down to Haman. After realizing that Mordecai disobeyed the king's decree, Haman became angry and vengeful. Although Haman was the king's right-hand man, his power wasn't enough to influence Mordecai to worship him. Consider this: if you are living a purpose-filled life for God, you too will become a target of hate. While opposition is always present, don't give up: rely on God's strength and strategies to defend your faith. You will make an impressionable impact on God's kingdom when you stand firm in your faith. Meanwhile, Haman made a solemn pledge to kill Mordecai, especially after learning his Jewish identity. Haman also vowed to destroy every Jew in the Persian Empire. Instead of respecting Mordecai's religion, Haman devised a plan and approached the king. Without mentioning Mordecai's name, Haman told the king that a certain man disobeyed his decree (Esther 3:6–8).

Are you careful to avoid things that will hinder your relationship with Christ? Why is maintaining a strong relationship with Christ important to you? Does your Holy-Spirit-filled life demonstrate that you are different from others in the world? If your lifestyle doesn't reflect Christ, then how are you making an impact in the world if you're like it? Besides, James 4:4 warns believers by saying that we are God's enemy when we love the things of the world. With that in mind, as followers of Christ, 2 Corinthians 6:14-17 is straightforward in saying that we must separate ourselves from anything or anyone that could lead us to sin. By the way, sin leads to isolation, which will eventually cause us to leave God. When we are entangled in worldly matters, we are misrepresenting God's kingdom.

Doesn't 1 Peter 1:16 boldly affirm that God is holy, so we should be holy? When you submit to God's leadership, people will see and know the difference between godliness and ungodliness by watching you. Christians who follow Christ are great influencers for God's kingdom. As indicated in Mark 16:17, believers have the power to perform miracles. Why? Because Christ dwells in us and we have the authority to cast out demons and heal the sick. As a result of this, John 14:12 says that because of our faith, we will perform greater miracles! Therefore, we must declare that our family, friends, and even strangers come out of darkness and into Christ's glorious kingdom. In fact, as a Christ influencer, it is written in Romans 4:17 that we have the authority to call things into existence that do not yet exist.

Moreover, Esther 3:8-10 states Haman continued with his malicious lies by asking the king to make a decree to annihilate the Jews. Haman's spirit of hatred caused him to seek revenge amongst the Jews. His act of violence almost caused devastation to the Jews and the nation itself. Haman told the king that he would deposit ten thousand talents of silver in the royal treasury if the Jews were eliminated. Unaware that Haman was from the lineage of the Amalekites, who hated the Jews, the careless king rejected Haman's money but implemented a decree to murder the Jews. After hearing about the decree to destroy the Jews, a deep sense of sorrow gripped Mordecai. In his distress, he entered the streets of the city and arrived in front of the king's palace, weeping loudly with tears flowing down his face. Once hearing that Mordecai was greatly grieved in his spirit, Esther sent her eunuch to speak with him. Mordecai told the eunuch about the death threat placed on the Jewish race in Persia. Then, Mordecai commanded the eunuch to tell Esther to approach the king immediately.

Esther Pushed Further into Her Purpose

Esther replied to Mordecai with great concern about going to see the king. She explained that according to Persian law, if you're not invited to the king's palace but go anyway, it will cost you your life. The response Esther gave Mordecai didn't please him. He said, "Just because you live in the palace, do not think for one moment that you won't die with the Jews. If you remain silent, the Lord will save the Jews, but you and your family will die." At that moment, Mordecai emphasized to Esther that the appointed time to be used by God was now! Then, Mordecai commanded Esther to take full advantage of her royal position. His electrifying message of compassion for the Jews propelled Esther to move further into her divine purpose. Esther didn't realize that her divine assignment was greater than being married to the wealthiest man in the world (Esther 4:11–14).

Esther's real purpose was to save the Jewish people within the city of Susa. It wasn't by happenstance that the Lord positioned her to be the next queen of Persia. Esther immediately accepted the assignment to save her people after receiving Mordecai's compelling message. Esther knew that she could possibly die because she didn't have permission to see the king. Nevertheless, Esther was willing to risk her life for the Jewish people. Do you believe with God's help that you can accomplish great things in your lifetime? Proverbs 16:3 declares that we can accomplish anything when we rely on God. Think about this: speaking with God first will also prevent unnecessary detours. The Lord will always provide a spiritual map of your assignment when you talk to him first. However, if you lack faith in fulfilling your assignment, ask God to allow you to see the vision as he sees it. The Lord will enlarge your vision so that you can complete his will. Once God expands your thinking, you will be surprised how innovative you are. You will also notice how compassionate you've become about fulfilling your assignment. By the way, your passion is the fuel that you will need to achieve your God-given purpose. By living out your divine purpose to the best of your ability, you must remember to glorify God. Ultimately, every decision that you make should please God. When you consult with God about your purpose, the possibilities are limitless!

Fasting, a Strategy for Fulfilling Your Purpose

Mordecai's unflinching faithfulness to God led Esther to ask him and the Jews to fast with her. Esther also made a vow to Mordecai that she would speak with the king after the fast was completed. Esther acknowledged that the Jews needed God's divine favor by calling a corporate fast with the Jewish community and Mordecai. Instead of being consumed with worry about Haman's death threat, Esther 4:16 says the Jews fasted for three days without any food or liquids. Do you believe that praying and fasting will allow you to hear God clearly? As believers, we can receive divine revelation about every assignment from God. When you read your Bible, you will notice that fasting was a common practice in ancient days. Fasting is a good spiritual discipline that we should always practice. Along with praying and fasting, Joshua 1:8 tells us to consistently study our Bible. Therefore, when we fast and pray, it's impossible to lose sight of what God has instructed us to do. To be successful at fasting, we must remember to depend on God's strength and not our own strength. Having faith in God's power is essential to fasting. However, failure is inevitable if we lack confidence in God.

Exodus 34:28 explains that the Lord will sustain us when we fast. According to the text, Moses did not eat or drink for forty days while he was with the Lord at Mount Sinai. Moses was fulfilling his divine purpose while he fasted forty days and forty nights. How did Moses go without eating and drinking for such a long time? Moses was able to endure because he was in the Lord's presence.

While fasting in the Lord's presence at Mount Sinai, the Lord gave Moses the famous Ten Commandments for the nation of Israel. These commandments were written with the Lord's fingers, as stated in Exodus 31:18. Also, in Exodus 25, while in the Lord's presence, Moses was told how to build a sanctuary. After reading this, we should be motivated to live a life of prayer and fasting. Why? Because both prayer and fasting are effective spiritual tools. Therefore, when we fast and pray, we must expect God to perform the phenomenal, the unthinkable.

Further, when the Jews were accused unjustly for a crime they didn't commit, they needed God to perform a miracle. The Jews humbled themselves, asked God for forgiveness of their sins, and expected God to move on their behalf. Without any reservations, the Jews placed their faith in the Lord, whom they could trust. The Jews understood that nothing is hidden from God's people when they pray and fast. If you had a life-or-death situation, would you take a bold stand for your faith? If not, why are you fearful? Second Timothy 1:7 says God has not given us the Spirit of fear, but we have power, love, and the ability to make sound decisions. We are also advised in Hebrews 11:6 that without faith, it's impossible to please God. James 1:7 also warns believers by saying that if we doubt God's ability, then we shouldn't expect anything from him. Instead of worrying or seeking the counsel of a fellow man, we must trust God. When we are confident in the Lord's authority, we are rewarded. The enemy is also defeated when we are persistent at being committed to God with a life of fasting and praying. Therefore, we are victorious over every situation because we have received divine strategies from the Lord.

Esther and Mordecai's Purpose Fulfilled

No matter what Haman, the enemy of the Jews, tried, the Jews believed that God was in control. As indicated in Proverbs 10:25, when the storms of life come, the wicked vanish, but the righteous will be kept safe forever. Proverbs 26:27 also says that whoever digs a pit for another man will surely fall into it. Taking this into account, the Jews were committed to the Lord; therefore, they received a favorable outcome. As a result of the Jews' worship for the Lord, their lives were extended. However, Haman was murdered, as stated in Esther 7:10, along with his ten sons, which is recorded in Esther 9:10. Surely, it was Esther's extraordinary faith in God that spared the lives of the Jews throughout the Persian Empire. Her uncompromising faith in God and her brave spirit were the keys to liberating her Jewish brothers and sisters.

Just as Esther fulfilled her purpose on Persian soil, so did Mordecai. The man of God became a very well-known leader with great political power within the Persian Empire. Having enormous favor with the king, Esther 10:3 says Mordecai became the second-highest government official throughout Persia. Mordecai also served as a loyal servant to the Jewish community. The Jews, as well as other nationalities throughout the empire, loved Mordecai. According to Esther 8:17, many of the nationalities professed to be Jews because they feared the Jewish people. We too can be like Mordecai, making an impact beyond our family and friends when we trust the Lord. The Lord can do extraordinary, unimaginable things through us if we allow him. As a Christian, you are an illuminator for Christ. Matthew 5:16 says it best: a righteous lifestyle is a weapon for Christians to let their light shine so that all men can believe that there is a Holy God. Thus, when our light shines, we glorify God!

Your Assignment Was Chosen Before Birth

> *I am the vine; you are the branches. If you remain in me and I in you, you will bear much fruit; apart from me you can do nothing. If you do not remain in me, you are like a branch that is thrown away and withers; such branches are picked up, thrown into the fire and burned. If you remain in me and my words remain in you, ask whatever you wish, and it will be done for you.*
>
> —JOHN 15:5-7

As an heir in God's kingdom, you have been given special privileges. Your benefits include an incredible opportunity to make a positive impact in the world. According to Galatians 4:7, as God's child, you have full access to his inheritance. Isn't it an honor that you have been chosen to shape the future for God's kingdom? With this in mind, may you cherish and embrace this amazing gift from the Lord. Are you aware of your kingdom benefits? To put it another way, God has created a special assignment just for you. That's right: the world is eagerly waiting for your unique contribution. As noted in Jeremiah 1:5, before you were conceived, the Lord chose a specific assignment for you. Can you believe that you were on the Lord's mind before your parents met? That being said, your life was carefully planned by the Lord. This makes your existence truly remarkable. Better yet, your existence is not a coincidence. In fact, you are precious to the Lord. He wants you to experience a life filled with love, joy, and purpose.

Are you ready to accept your kingdom assignment? Perhaps you don't feel spiritually mature to accomplish the task. Maybe you're in disbelief that God has chosen you. Think about this: since God chose you, he has already qualified you for the job! Now, you must collaborate with Christ to receive divine instructions about your assignment. As you collaborate with Christ, it's essential that you pay attention. When you are focused on God, you are open to exploring new possibilities and perspectives. Partnering with God will transform your thinking. When you have the mindset of

Christ, you're an innovative thinker with fresh, creative ideas. You will also achieve the results that Christ expects of you through this collaboration. Christ will ultimately empower you to strive for the greatness that already exists within you. To fulfill such greatness, one must rely on the guidance of the Holy Spirit. Do you trust the Lord as your pilot to direct you? If so, the Lord will give you strategies to overcome any obstacles that may arise. According to Proverbs 16:3, individuals who share their plans with the Lord are guaranteed success. Keeping this in mind, when you trust God, you can expect to be an undefeated champion. Anything that bears the Lord's name must prosper.

Stay Connected to the Vine, Jesus Christ

Furthermore, in John 15:5, Jesus Christ provides a simple formula for success in the kingdom of God. Christ does this by presenting a story using the imagery of vines and branches. Within this text, Christ illustrates that he is the vine and believers are the branches. Jesus uses this metaphor to emphasize the importance of believers staying connected to him to bear fruit. Having said this, maintaining a close relationship with the Lord is an important aspect of bearing fruit and growing in the Christian faith. A close relationship with Christ brings about personal transformation and growth. Christians who grow closer to Christ are more compassionate, empathic, and sensitive toward others. By embracing these Christ-like qualities, we inspire others to seek the truth of God's love and salvation.

Moreover, vines play a significant role in outdoor living. Vines enhance gardens with their magnificent and vibrant yet sometimes subtle colors. Their flexibility and multifaceted role allow them to provide shade and transform structures into something remarkable and beautiful. Despite their diversity, vines need specific care before they blossom, just like believers. With that said, branches can't survive without the support of a vine. Branches are weak and unable to support themselves. This same truth applies to believers. Without God, Christians will not survive. As believers, we are fragile. We need a lot of care from the vine, our Lord Christ, who is our source of strength and support. Just as vines enhance gardens with their vibrant colors, our connection to Jesus adds beauty and purpose to our lives. Thus, let us strive to stay connected to Christ so we may flourish in our faith, just like the vines in our gardens.

Moreover, fruit must get nutrients from vines to thrive, which is another important function of vines. But if the vine is unhealthy, the fruit will not develop. This can ultimately reduce the yield and quality of the harvest. In addition, nutrient deficiencies can make the fruit more susceptible to diseases and pests. Therefore, the health of the vine is critical to the fruit's success. That being said, vines need time to grow and mature. In order to bear fruit, they need to be exposed to the right amount of sunlight, nutrients, and water. However, once the vine has grapes, the lifespan of a grapevine can last many years.

On the other hand, Christians also need time to grow spiritually in order to bear fruit. Because of this, we must seek the Lord's help. Without the Lord's guidance, it's impossible to be productive in his kingdom. Bearing fruit in the kingdom ultimately glorifies God. By investing in Christ now, we will reap a bountiful harvest for years to come.

Although the grapevine planting and bearing fruit in God's kingdom is somewhat similar, both will require patience and proper care. To assist us with this process, listed below are some important components for both planting grapevines and bearing fruit in God's kingdom. If we are going to fulfill our purpose, then we must adhere to these principles, which include Soaking in God's Presence (Soaking Vines Before Planting), Christ the Holy Soil (Vines and Good Soil), Jesus Christ Our Support System (Vines Need Support), Trimming and Pruning Makes Us Like Christ (Vines are Healthy when Trimmed and Pruned), and Christ the Lord of Harvest (Vines Are Fully Developed).

Soaking in God's Presence
(Soaking Vines Before Planting)

Soaking in the Lord's presence is required to accomplish our God-given assignment. Strategies are revealed when we spend time praying and studying God's word. John 15:4 clearly says that if we are going to bear fruit, then staying connected to Christ is essential. When we fail to remain faithful to God, we will not produce anything for his kingdom. The best way to stay connected to the Lord is to spend quality time with him. As explained in 1 Thessalonians 5:17, we must get in a habit of praying often. In addition to praying, the only way to obey God is to do what Joshua 1:8 advises: meditate on the Scriptures day and night. According to 2 Timothy 3:16–17, when we study our Bible, we become equipped to do God's work. As a result of combining prayer and reading our Bible on a regular basis, we shall fulfill God's will for our life.

The term "soaking" is also used when planting grapevines. Before planting grapevines, they should be thoroughly saturated in water. Once the vine is planted, there must be some type of water system in place.[1] Having a water system is beneficial to the health of the vine. A water plan in place ensures that the plants are getting enough water to reach their full potential. Water is necessary for the growth of a flourishing, beautiful grapevine. The use of a soaking hose is an efficient way to water the grapevines. This method allows water to directly reach the roots, ensuring the health and vitality of your plants. However, one must be careful because too much water can damage the roots of the vine. Hence, providing the right amount of water without overdoing it is crucial.

Furthermore, both humans and plants need water to live a healthy and productive life. In the same way vines require water to survive, Christians must also immerse themselves in the presence of the life giver, God. By doing this, we will accomplish great things because of our commitment to the Lord. Are you confident that you will reach your full potential without God? The writer in Psalm 42:1–2 describes how "his soul thirsts for the living

---

1. Taylor, *Taylor's Encyclopedia of Gardening*, 25.

God." The psalmist compared his dependence on God to a deer that relied on water for survival. Having said this, we too must acknowledge that God is important. When God is our priority, we will adopt the same attitude as the psalmist. Otherwise, like plants, we will die without the living water, which is God.

Christ the Holy Soil
(Vines and Good Soil)

The next component to bearing fruit, which is also vital to both humans and vines, is soil. All living beings on the planet rely on soil for survival. Good quality soil is imperative to the survival of plants and humans. For example, a vine that has healthy, strong roots throughout the first year could possibly develop and produce hearty fruit. On the other hand, while vines are flexible and resilient, the soil must be well drained to produce fruit. For instance, when the soil is well drained, it retains heat. Having warm soil not only enhances vine growth but speeds up the ripening process, resulting in more flavorful grapes. Additionally, adding the right amount of nutrients to the soil is crucial for stimulating plant growth. It is also important for holes in the soil to be very deep and wide before planting the grapevine. The soil should also be damp and loose, providing the necessary moisture for the roots to flourish.[2] Maintaining the appropriate pH level in the soil is also necessary for the development of the vine. The ideal soil pH level ranges from 5.5 to 7.0.[3] It is essential to monitor the soil's pH to ensure the overall health and productivity of the vine. Another critical factor for a long-lasting, healthy vine is the plant site. The plant site must receive plenty of sunlight to facilitate the fruit growth on the grapevine.

In the same way plants require good quality soil for growth, so it is important for believers to be planted in God. When we are rooted in God, who represents good soil, we will receive the

---

2. Cox, *From Vines to Wines*, 44–46.
3. Taylor, *Taylor's Encyclopedia of Gardening*, 24.

proper nutrients to thrive in the kingdom. Therefore, we must be determined to stay connected to Christ. John 15:5 reminds believers, "Apart from [Christ, we] can do nothing." When we are detached from the vine (Christ), this hinders our spiritual growth and limits our ability to bear fruit. Taking this into account, without the power of God, will you effectively succeed at fulfilling your divine purpose? No, because God is the creator of the vision. Now then, keep your relationship with God strong and your life will be meaningful and fulfilling. By doing this, you will gain insight, strength, and strategies for your kingdom assignment. Therefore, because you have aligned your life with the Scripture, having a bright and successful future is God's promise to you, as shown in Jeremiah 29:11.

Did you notice what the Lord said about your future in the above sentence? In case you didn't, because of God's unconditional love and grace, you have favor. Deuteronomy 28:6 states that the Lord will bless everything you do. However, you must fully obey the Lord. Making a commitment to reading your Bible is a sure way to follow God's commandments. After all, reading the Bible consistently will help you make better choices. As noted in Psalm 119:105, we are instructed to let the word of God guide us, which is the light that illuminates our path. Psalm 37:31 also says we will avoid taking the wrong path when we allow God's teachings to guide us each day.

Isaiah 55:8 says it best: "The Lord says: 'My thoughts and my ways are not like yours'" (CEV). With this in mind, we must get in the habit of synchronizing our life and our thoughts with the Lord's Holy Scriptures. We are reminded in Romans 12:2 that our minds must be transformed. In other words, changing the way we think is a powerful way for God to reshape and transform our lives. Once we allow the Lord to redirect our thinking, we will learn how to please him. As a result, our prayers become more focused on his will instead of our own desires.

Jesus Christ Our Support System
(Vines Need Support)

Another important process that contributes to the healthy development of vines and humans is a strong support system. Grapevines require the support of trellises, fences, or walls. As climbing plants, vines need a support structure during the first year of planting. Given that certain vines tend to grow upward, support structures are necessary. With this in mind, vines should be at least five feet apart when planting.[4] This will allow the vines to spread out and ascend toward the sun. As the vines climb upward, they will have an opportunity to develop properly. Vines can also adapt to most environmental conditions. In addition, the vine will grow tremendously in rich soil and plenty of water.

Just like vines, we too must have a strong support system. As believers, our support system is Jesus Christ. Failure is definite if we don't rely on Christ while pursuing our divine assignment. Without an intimate relationship with Christ, we are like the useless branch described in John 15:6. When we become detached from the vine (Christ), we are weak and ineffective in God's kingdom. Hence, our ability to bear fruit, serve others, and make a lasting impact is diminished. Thus, if you are going to bear fruit, you must be determined to stay attached to the vine, Christ. His direction, strength, and support are unmatched. As the true vine, Christ is authentic and not a counterfeit. Therefore, Christ as the vine nourishes and sustains his children and empowers them to grow spiritually and to have a fruitful life.

Trimming and Pruning Makes Us Like Christ
(Vines Are Healthy when Trimmed and Pruned)

To ensure rapid growth, grapevines must be trimmed and pruned. Trimming increases vine productivity and strengthens the vines. In addition to trimming the vines, the plant must also go through a pruning process. The method of pruning is to

---

4. Taylor, *Taylor's Encyclopedia of Gardening*, 29.

remove the dead branches. The grapevine will continue to grow if pruned properly. Pruning also plays a vital role in the plant's beauty. Pruning the vines, however, can be a very difficult task to maintain. Nonetheless, neglected vines won't produce fruit if they are not pruned and trimmed regularly. From time to time, vines will get out of control. When this happens, vines need to be redirected so they can continue in the right direction. Redirection is necessary for the vine. Ultimately, the vine must climb toward the sunlight. The amount of sun the grapevine receives will determine how fast the vine grows.

Isn't it quite interesting that Christ compares the church to one of the fastest-growing plants in the world? This lets us know that when we pursue God instead of our own interests, the kingdom is expanded. However, to be productive in God's kingdom, we must go through the trimming and pruning process. The process involves eliminating anything or anyone that doesn't belong in our lives. The goal of this process is shapes us to be like Christ, so we can bear fruit.

Christ the Lord of Harvest
(Vines Are Fully Developed)

Finally, the deep colorful grapes on the vine are ready for harvesting. After harvesting, the grapevines will appear to be mature. Even so, the gardener must use caution before removing the grapes from the vine. The gardener should avoid removing the fruit from the vine because of the size or color. While the grapes may be plump with beautiful bold colors, this does not mean the fruit is ripe. Fruit can be deceitful, so beware. Then again, even the smallest grapes are ready to be taken from the vine. Before removing the grapes, the gardener should sample a few grapes from different areas of the vine. If the grapes are sweet, then more than likely, the fruit can be removed from the vine. However, the gardener should leave the grapes on the vine if the fruit isn't mature. These same principles also apply to God's sons and daughters. Unfortunately, if we are not spiritually mature, we will not accomplish our God-given assignment. Our divine assignments can be better understood when we are mature in Christ. Our best course of action is to examine why we haven't grown closer to the Son as quickly as we should have.

Furthermore, as the Lord's children, we are commanded to bear fruit. Sadly, when we fail to bear fruit, we are violating our Father's commandments. Are you fulfilling the call that God has placed on your life? If you're not bearing fruit, you're not productive; therefore, you won't make a difference in God's kingdom. Taking this into account, because you are the Lord's child, Galatians 1:15–16 says you have been given a divine assignment. To fulfill your assignment, you will need courage, faith, and commitment to God. With these spiritual tools, you are better equipped to navigate any challenges that come your way. That being said, by embracing your assignment, you will experience true joy that comes from aligning your life with God's intended plan.

On the other hand, if you have diligently followed each stage of the grapevine growth process, then you are bearing fruit. You are like a mature, healthy grapevine which produces plenty of fruit. Having done this, you are following Matthew 5:16: "Let your light so shine before men, that they may see your good works and glorify your Father in heaven" (NKJV). By doing this, people will want a relationship with God. Surely, this will glorify your Father in heaven. According to John 15:8, you are pleasing the Lord by being his disciple and using your gifts and influence to serve him. Therefore, while fulfilling your kingdom assignment, remain focused and take advantage of every opportunity to spread the good news of Jesus Christ.

Power Points on Knowing God's Purpose for Your Life

God's faithful hand must nurture the preeminent greatness that's on your life. When you follow God's leadership, you will have the passion and tenacity to execute ingenious ideas. A partnership with God will help you become more confident in yourself. Therefore, whatever you're hoping for, Ephesians 3:20 says, "Now all glory to God, who is able, through his mighty power at work within us, to accomplish infinitely more than we might ask or think" (NLT). With this in mind, if you are bold enough to believe God, you will be unstoppable in doing what God has called you to do. Listed below are six Power Points called P.U.R.S.U.E., which will help you stay focused on fulfilling your purpose while doing great things for God's kingdom.

P ersistence is vital when you are living out your divine purpose because the assignment won't be easy. As long as you remain in prayer, you will overcome every obstacle. Therefore, be strong and put on the full armor of God. Always remember what Philippians 4:13 says, you can do all things because Christ empowers you to do so. God is the navigator of the assignment; don't let go of his unchanging hand (Proverbs 3:5–7; Joshua 1:5–7; Ephesians 6:10–18).

U nderstand how to accomplish your assignment. The first step to believing in your assignment is to visualize it. Be eager and consistent about seeking God for revelation concerning the assignment. Ask God to expand your intellectual capacity. Once you believe, you will have clarity on how to accomplish your assignment. When you receive God's instructions, don't delay—react quickly to what he said (Proverbs 4:1–5; 28:19; Habakkuk 2:2–3; Hosea 4:6).

R emain focused. Commit to Christ and you will be successful in achieving your purpose. Remove negative people. They don't see your vision. Some people will convince you that God didn't call you to greatness. Do not doubt God. The Bible warns that if you are filled with unbelief, don't expect to receive anything from God. When your faith is inconsistent, you can't be loyal to God or fulfill your purpose (Joshua 1:6-7; Psalms 37:23; 51:6; Proverbs 3:4).

S pecific directions from God are necessary to thrive in a life filled with purpose. Have confidence in God's leadership. He has confidence in you! When you follow God's strategic plan, you have the capacity to go above and beyond the norm (Psalm 37:3-4; Psalm 147:5-6; Psalm 119:133-34; 1 Samuel 2:9).

U nite with God. Maintain your momentum with God. Stay connected to God by reading your Bible. It's your responsibility to know God's intended plan for your life. Anytime you collaborate with God, your future looks bright and prosperous. God will do the impossible if you would just believe (Isaiah 40:31; Romans 8:28; Psalm 139:13-15; Jeremiah 29:11; Joshua 1:8).

E mbrace the Lord's perspective regarding your assignment. As you fulfill your purpose, trust God and you will receive groundbreaking ideas that will have a lasting impact. Wait on God with an expectation of receiving his promises (1 Peter 2:9; Psalm 145:13; 1 Thessalonians 2:12; Romans 8:31).

4

Secrets to Applying God's Wisdom to Your Life

Then Daniel returned to his house and explained the matter to his friends Hananiah, Mishael, and Azariah. He urged them to plead for mercy from the God of heaven concerning this mystery; so that he and his friends might not be executed with the rest of the wise men of Babylon.

—DANIEL 2:17–18

The King's Forgotten Dream

ONE NIGHT, KING NEBUCHADNEZZAR's sleep was interrupted by a very disturbing dream. This happened during the second year of his reign as the king of Babylon. The king knew that the dream conveyed an important message. Yet, his inability to recall the dream terrified him. Due to fear and lack of insight to interpret his dream, the king commanded the wise men to come to his royal palace. The king expected the wise men to interpret his dream. Unfortunately, the wise men could not accurately translate the meaning of the king's dream. In fact, the wise men pleaded with the king, saying that his request was impossible. Their failure to describe the dream caused the king to become angry. Because of their incompetent behavior, Daniel 2:1-15 says the king proclaimed a death sentence on all the wise men in Babylon. Whenever the king pronounced judgment against anyone, it was irrevocable. As a result, all the wise men received a death sentence. Now that the king's decree was in place, the king's commander, Arioch, sought to execute Daniel, his friends, and the wise men of Babylon. Nevertheless, when Daniel saw his executioner, Arioch, he remained calm. With a humble spirit, Daniel asked Arioch, "Why was the king's decree so cruel and urgent?" Daniel realized the situation was critical after hearing Arioch's explanation of the king's death threat.

Lack Wisdom? Ask God

When confronted with a crisis, how do you respond? Crisis situations are best handled with a delicate response. Your response to critical situations will determine the outcome. Ultimately, we need God's insight in every situation we face. Since we are heirs to God's kingdom, we should make every attempt to understand God. Having wisdom will guide our choices and actions. The ability to make wise decisions is critical. More importantly, when we pray and receive God's wisdom, we can make informed decisions and live fulfilling lives. Proverbs 15:8 explains that the Lord enjoys hearing the prayers of the righteous. We are also encouraged by Psalm 25:14 which reassures us that the Lord confides in those that fear him.

Having said this, seeking God's counsel will always eliminate anxiety. This is why it is written in James 1:5 that we should ask God for assistance when we lack direction and wisdom. Of course, we must have faith in God's wisdom. According to Proverbs 8:11, gaining wisdom is more important than having beautiful gemstones. Therefore, no one or anything can compare to God's wisdom. Proverbs 3:13 says it best: blessed is the person who has godly wisdom. Proverbs 8:3 also declares that a person who has wisdom has life and favor with God. Hence, when we choose to live right before the Lord, Psalm 84:11 states that the Lord doesn't withhold anything from us.

With this in mind, the Lord will give us peace, courage, and joy once we talk to him about our concerns. Unlike the furious king who placed his hope in men, when we seek the Lord, we will not be disappointed. Do you believe in God's wisdom? Notice I said God's wisdom and not your own wisdom. The wisdom of God exceeds our intellect. Although we are created in God's image, our knowledge is very limited, whereas God's knowledge is limitless. When we have divine wisdom from God, the outcome is always favorable.

God's Wisdom Cancels Fear

Daniel was at a turning point in his life. He had to decide if he was going to trust God or panic about his execution. As a young prophet, Daniel, with spiritual discernment, chose to trust God. Instead of focusing on the king's threats, the young Hebrew concentrated on the Lord. Daniel's uncompromising faith in God surpassed any doubt or fear regarding the decree from the pagan king. For this reason, Daniel stood on the passage 2 Timothy 1:7, which says God has not given us the spirit of fear; instead, we have power, love, and a sound mind.

Are you reluctant about fulfilling your God-given assignment because you're afraid of failure? Whenever there is fear, then failure is certain. As stated in John 14:27, we have God's peace; therefore, we shouldn't operate in fear. When we rest in God's peace, we are not troubled but strengthened during every challenge. Because of this, having God's peace will control the way we think and feel. We are also reminded by the apostle Paul in Philippians 4:7 that God's peace goes far beyond anything we can imagine. Keeping this in mind, God's peace is always available to us. However, we must understand that only God can give us the peace we need. Once we realize this, we can do what Proverbs 3:5–6 says: don't trust your own judgement but depend on God.

Furthermore, are you aware that the spirit of fear is a silent killer? Often, life situations can knock us down. Instead of getting up and putting our trust in God, we become terrified and defeated. Sadly, we become paralyzed when we allow the spirit of fear to rest upon us. The spirit of fear is like a crippling disease that prevents us from believing in the supremacy of God. Hence, if fear has gripped your life, then fear controls you, not God. Consider this: you serve a powerless god when you allow fear to control you. When you have the spirit of fear, you are incapable of obeying God because you have no confidence in God's power and authority.

When you have the capacity to believe God, the spirit of fear is not an option. When you trust God, you have the power to defeat the enemy. Now then, because of your faith, you are courageous rather than timid. Not to mention, you are victorious over every circumstance despite what the situation looks like. As a matter of fact, the Bible guarantees that God is a sustainer and will deliver us from any situation. His inspired word also provides guidance, hope, and comfort in times of distress. Having said this, God's word is a firm foundation that we can build our lives on. Furthermore, when we study our Bible, we will receive spiritual nourishment, which fills our hearts and minds with divine truth. Therefore, let us embrace God's word. As we do this, his word will shape our lives and bring us closer to him. By growing closer to God, we can live a life that honors him. Once this happens, we will have true fulfillment and purpose in life.

Execution Delayed While Daniel Seeks God

Meanwhile, Daniel decided to meet with the angry king. When Daniel saw the king, he told him that he could interpret the dream, but he needed more time. At Daniel's request, the king allowed him more time to consult with his God. Unlike the wise men, Daniel and his friends received favor from the Lord, and their execution was delayed. The four Hebrews stood together in spite of the king's death threat. According to Daniel 2:16–18, the young men prayed, asking the Lord to reveal the king's mysterious dream. The Hebrews were confident that the Lord didn't bring them to Babylon to be executed. Daniel and his friends understood that God had great plans for their lives. They knew their purpose, and it was to serve and glorify God in the pagan culture of Babylon. Do you have friends who are eager to receive divine revelation from God? Having friends that hear the divine voice of God is valuable. If you don't have spiritual friendships, ask the Lord to help you find friends who are willing to listen and obey him.

The Bible says there is tremendous power when two or more people are united in their faith. Matthew 18:20 says Christ is present when believers agree with one another. That's right, the Lord honors agreement. In fact, John 16:23 proclaims that when Christians pray together in unity, asking anything in God's name, they shall receive it. However, anyone who has a desire to obey God must learn how to wait on his timing. As we wait on the Lord, because of our patience, we will receive his power, mercy, and his favor.

Daniel and his friends understood the principle of seeking and waiting on the Lord. Their strong faith in God's word led them to believe Luke 1:37, which says, "For with God nothing shall be impossible" (KJV). Is your faith like Daniel and his friends? Perhaps you have lost faith in God when you experienced a difficult situation. The Lord has the solution for your impossible situations. Are you willing to trust God? If not, I am praying that your confidence in the Lord's ability will increase. Instead of doubting God, when you hear his gentle voice, you will quickly trust and obey him.

With God's Wisdom, Daniel Interprets the Dream

The powerful effect of unified prayer is also repeated in Daniel 2:17–19. As the four Hebrews invoked God's presence, standing in agreement, the Lord heard the prayers of Daniel, Hananiah, Mishael, and Azariah. The young men believed Jeremiah 33:3, which says that the Lord will reveal things that are beyond our understanding when we talk to him. Because the Lord is faithful, he revealed to Daniel the meaning of the king's mysterious dream. Then Daniel, with great admiration, praised the one and only living God. While worshiping God, Daniel acknowledged the Lord's sovereignty, his faithfulness, and God's divine counsel. Daniel's gratitude continues as he acknowledges that only God discloses "the deep and hidden things of life."

Having received the revelation about the dream, Daniel, without hesitation, went to visit the king. Filled with prophetic insight, the young Hebrew told the king that the God of Israel has explained the meaning of the mysterious dream (Daniel 2:20–43). At once, Daniel began describing the dream to the king, saying that the beautiful, large statue that the king saw in the dream symbolized four kingdoms that will control the world. The head of the statue was pure gold, which represented the kingdom of Babylon. The chest and the arms of the statue were silver, which symbolized the Medo-Persian Empire. The belly and the thighs of the statue were bronze, which represented the Grecian Empire. Lastly, the legs and the feet of the statue were iron and clay, which points to the Roman Empire. Then, after telling the king what each part of the statue represented, Daniel said, "Although the Lord has given you dominion and power over the earth, your kingdom will be crushed into pieces by the Medo-Persian Empire." Daniel then told the king that the Roman Empire would destroy the Medo-Persian Empire, along with the Grecian Empire. Daniel also advised the king that during this time, God's kingdom would be established. Therefore, because God reigns over the earth, Daniel 2:44 says his kingdom will annihilate all these kingdoms. That being said, God's kingdom will last forever.

God's Wisdom Is Valuable

As described in Daniel 1:17, the four Hebrews were given intelligence and wisdom by the Lord. The text also says the Lord gave Daniel divine understanding of various kinds of visions and dreams. Daniel's profound insight and faith in God provided hope for the king and all the wise men of Babylon. Isn't it incredible how the sovereign Lord allowed Daniel to interpret another man's dream? We too have been given the privilege to join our thoughts with the Lord's thoughts. First Corinthians 2:16 states, "We have the mind of Christ." Having the mind of Christ simply means that the Spirit of God lives in us. The Holy Spirit is the source that leads us toward the right path. But we must trust and yield to his gentle whispers for guidance. When we are open to the direction of the Holy Spirit, our ideas, dreams, and desires can be fulfilled. Given that the Holy Spirit dwells in us, we should live a life that glorifies God. Having said this, when we yield to the Spirit of God, we are not influenced by the world but by the Holy Spirit. By following the Holy Spirit, we will discover his intended purpose and plan for our lives. Then, he will equip us with the necessary tools to accomplish his will.

Moreover, are you interested in finding out how to handle perplexing situations in your life? If this is your desire, take some time and study the book of Daniel. The Lord will make all things clear to you when you talk to him. However, you must believe that when you pray, the Lord will answer. A life of prayer will keep you rooted in your faith. By praying, you will learn how to keep your mind, heart, and eyes on Christ instead of allowing your situations to consume you.

Finally, if you remain committed to seeking God's wisdom, you will receive strategies on how to be an effective problem-solver. The key to receiving divine insight from God is to make him first above everything. When you have God's wisdom, nothing matches receiving the divine counsel of God. Having God's wisdom, as noted in Proverbs 3:2, brings blessings, favor, riches, and a long life of peace. Therefore, when the Lord does reveal his wisdom to you, don't forget to praise him. The Lord is worthy of all the glory because of his unwavering commitment, patience, and ever-present love for us. Even when we are not faithful, the Lord is always faithful. His dedication to us extends beyond our faithfulness. This should be a reminder that we are never alone in our struggles because of the Lord's faithfulness. Let us therefore embrace our faithful Father who will always be by our side, guiding us with love and compassion.

King David's Desire to Please God

But now your kingdom will not endure; the LORD has sought out a man after his own heart and appointed him ruler of his people, because you have not kept the LORD's command.

—1 SAMUEL 13:14

Amongst all of Israel's kings, Solomon's father David was the greatest. David ruled as Israel's king for more than forty years, according to 1 Kings 2:11. David, however, made many mistakes as Israel's second king. Despite his mistakes, David was a man after God's heart. He was also a man who was sincere in acknowledging his sins. David's true repentance was demonstrated when the prophet Nathan confronted him about his adulterous behavior with Bathsheba. David's unlawful act not only included sleeping with another man's wife (Bathsheba), but he also murdered her husband. After killing her husband, David married Bathsheba. She became pregnant and gave birth to their son. However, because of his sin, the prophet warned David that his son would die. The prophecy was fulfilled in 2 Samuel 12:18, when David's son died.

David was devastated when his son died. Although God's decision caused David great distress, he never left God. Instead, he cried out to the Lord. Realizing he was undeserving of the Lord's mercy, he confessed his sin and asked for forgiveness. As noted in Psalm 51, David acknowledged his sin by saying, "Lord, I am aware of my sin, and my behavior was evil in your sight." David entreats the Lord further by admitting that his sinful nature started at birth, the moment his mother conceived him. While David is not excusing his wrongful behavior against God; rather, he is saying that because of his sinful nature, he would more than likely do evil. Nevertheless, David admits the Lord desired faithfulness while he was yet in his mother's womb. Because of this, David expressed that even in his mother's womb, he was taught to fear God. After taking ownership of his sin, David begged the Lord not to leave him and to forgive his transgressions. He closed his prayer by asking the Lord to give him wisdom on how to live a life of holiness. David knew he couldn't be loyal to God until he was taught how to obey God.

Can you relate to David's rebellious behavior? Sure, you can. As human beings, we have all struggled with some form of sin. Many of us have a desire to do right by God. Yet, it's impossible because of our sinful nature, according to Romans 7:18. In fact, the apostle Paul says it best in Romans 7:24: "What a wretched man I am!" In other words, Paul boldly proclaims that even when we want to do good, it's impossible because sin resides in us. Now then, because of our sinful nature, Galatians 5:17 declares that the flesh and the Spirit will always be at war with each other. That said, we must choose to live a life led by the Spirit of God and not by the flesh. A life lived by the Spirit will prevent us from giving in to our sinful desires. Having said this, the only way to overcome the conflict between the Spirit and the flesh is to hate what God hates and love what he loves.

Furthermore, when we understand that sin separates us from God, we are more likely to confess our sins. Sin is offensive to the Lord, for it is written in Habakkuk 1:13 that the Lord's eyes are too pure to look at sinful behavior, nor will the Lord tolerate our wickedness. As a result of our sin, Isaiah 59:2 affirms that the Lord will reject us, and he will not listen to our prayers. There is hope, though; Psalm 66:18 assures us by saying the Lord will hear our prayers when we confess our sins. Ephesians 4:30 also states that we should do everything in our power to avoid grieving the Holy Spirit. Consider this: our ungodly behavior grieves the Holy Spirit. In order to avoid grieving the Holy Spirit, we should stop doing what God doesn't like and obey him. To ensure that we are obeying God's commandments, we must be persistent with following the Scriptures. When we refuse to be separated from God, then sin does not rule us—God does.

God's Promise to David's Descendants

Before David's death, the God of Abraham made him a promise. The Lord told David in 2 Samuel 7:16 that his descendants would always rule as Israel's king. Jeremiah 23:5 also confirms that the Lord will choose an honest king from David's descendants, a king who is wise and rules with justice. That being said, the legacy of David would continue but only if his descendants remained faithful to God. Just as David and his descendants were not exempt from worshiping God, neither are we. When we keep the Lord's commandments, Deuteronomy 7:9 says that the Lord is faithful and will extend his covenant to a thousand generations for those who love him. Unlike man's promises, the Lord's promises are trustworthy. As we make God a priority, we can be certain that we will receive all his blessings. We are told in Proverbs 3:33 that the Lord blesses the home of the righteous; therefore, God must be first in our lives. It is also written in Deuteronomy 28:1–2 that the Lord's blessings will follow us when we obey him. Psalm 30:5 explains that while the Lord's anger toward us may be brief, his favor will last a lifetime. Proverbs 3:4 says that following God's commands is the key to having favor with God and man. Having said this, we should always praise the Lord because his devotion, mercy, and love toward us are unmatched. Keeping this in mind, the Lord is looking for people who are loyal, upright in heart, generous, courageous, caring, and steadfast in their faith.

It is therefore imperative that you remove everything that hinders you and your children from becoming ambassadors of Christ. Of course, this can only be achieved when you have a kingdom-legacy mindset. When you have a kingdom mindset, your worship for Christ is intentional. Worshiping Christ with purpose demonstrates that you will declare his power and follow his decrees. Because of your love for God, you will inspire your children to serve him. Since your children serve God, they will in turn tell the next generation about God. As the legacy of Christ is passed down to your family, Psalm 78:4–6 points out that because you taught your children God's law, the children who are not yet born will know God. As a result, they will not only know God, but they will also trust him and keep his commandments. Therefore, Romans 6:23 clearly states that the greatest gift we can pass down to our family is eternal life, which is given by Jesus Christ our Lord.

David also recognized that our everlasting, faithful God thinks in terms of generations. David understood that a relationship with God is the foundation for leaving a godly legacy. For this reason, David commanded his son Solomon to obey God when he became Israel's king. He knew that Solomon would be cared for, loved, and protected if he followed God. David also remembered what the Lord said about Solomon. In 2 Samuel 7:15, the Lord said to David, "My love for Solomon will never change." Therefore, David told Solomon, "Be loyal to God and you will succeed in everything you do." After receiving his father's advice, Solomon obeyed his father and served the Lord wholeheartedly. As we read the story of Solomon and David, we are reminded of God's loyalty and unchanging love towards us. Just as God made a vow to always love Solomon, he also promises to love and care for his children throughout every generation.

Solomon Asks for Wisdom

As the king of Israel, Solomon realized that God had given him a great responsibility. One night, after sacrificing a thousand burnt offerings at Gibeon, a place of worship, Solomon fell asleep. While sleeping, Solomon had a dream. In the dream, the Lord said, "Solomon, ask me for anything and I will give it to you." Solomon humbled himself, according to 1 Kings 3:4–9, and said, "Lord, help me to accomplish your will." Solomon wasn't ashamed to admit that he didn't know how to fulfill his assignment as Israel's king. Do you feel inexperienced like Solomon? Are you having difficulty doing what the Lord has told you to do? How do you feel about the assignment that the Lord has given you? From time to time, the Lord will give you an assignment that isn't familiar to you. Do not panic. It is the Lord's desire that you rely exclusively on him. Think about this: if your teacher gave you a difficult assignment, would you ask for help? Or would you attempt to complete the assignment without help and receive a failing grade? Prayerfully, you will ask your teacher for assistance. Or, even better, do as Solomon did: humble yourself and ask the Lord how to do your assignment. Asking the Lord for guidance on any assignment assures complete success!

Now then, we have faith in God, and he will never disappoint us when we humble ourselves under his leadership. Actually, a person who walks in humility has the Lord's attention. In fact, 1 Peter 5:5 explains the importance of adopting a humble attitude. The verse warns believers that the Lord hates arrogance, but he gives grace to the one who is humble. Therefore, when believers have humility, they have empathy, understanding, and are willing to serve and listen to others. Proverbs 22:4 also confirms that having humility and fearing the Lord are sure paths to receiving respect and a good life.

Solomon did not seek pleasures for himself. Instead, he sought God's wisdom on how to be Israel's king. Israel was comprised of numerous people who had different personalities and diverse cultural backgrounds. Has the Lord entrusted you with a multifaceted assignment? Does your calling consist of working with people who have different cultural backgrounds? The Lord's kingdom is very diverse. As God's chosen vessel, it's critical that you understand the population that you are assigned to. If you don't know how to interact with people from different backgrounds and cultures, ask God for help. The Lord will give you guidance on helping people who don't look or behave like you. Despite your differences, the number-one goal of your assignment is to invite people to follow God.

The Lord was pleased with Solomon. The young king was more concerned about God's kingdom than his own kingdom. It was Solomon's desire to discern between right and wrong. What about you? What's more important, your personal interests or the

Lord's affairs? Have you made a commitment to God to complete your assignment, as Solomon did? If so, then you are following Proverbs 10:8, which states that a wise person is willing to learn, listen, and follow God's instructions. As a matter of fact, Ecclesiastes 2:26 says that individuals who delight themselves in the Lord have wisdom and joy. Another important point made regarding wisdom is in Ecclesiastes 7:19. The passage says that a person with wisdom is more powerful than ten leaders in a city. Therefore, true power lies not in the title or the position of the person but in the wisdom that one possesses to make informed choices.

Furthermore, Solomon was so sincere in pleasing the Lord that it was impossible for the Lord to reject his request. The Lord honored Solomon by granting his request. Bearing this in mind, the Lord is more inclined to fulfill our requests when we genuinely seek to please him. The Lord empowered Solomon by blessing him with great insight. As a result of having great insight, Solomon could make intelligent decisions. Throughout his lifetime, Solomon was known as the wisest man in the world. He was an effective leader who could articulate with profound wisdom. For example, in 1 Kings 4:34, Solomon's captivating personality and wisdom inspired people to travel across the world to hear his wise teachings. Do you speak with wisdom from God? It is said in Proverbs 10:23 that a man with understanding has wisdom. Therefore, the influence of a wise person can inspire others to make a positive impact within their family, community, and society. Are your peers eager to hear the wisdom that God has given you? I hope that your family and friends are excited to hear divine insight from God. When you share God's wisdom, this should motivate the people around you to seek the Lord for guidance during exciting and difficult times.

With this in mind, wisdom from God is essential. Although many Christians lack God's wisdom, they fail to seek his guidance. The Bible clearly encourages believers to ask God to fill them with wisdom and discernment. The Scripture that comes to mind is Proverbs 2:6, which says we will receive the Lord's wisdom when we seek him. Ecclesiastes 2:14 also says wisdom is like having good eyes with 20/20 vision. For this reason, the wise have vision and know where they are going. On the other hand, the absence of wisdom will surely cause a foolish person to stumble.

Humility Brings Honor

Furthermore, when Solomon became the king of Israel, the Lord was delighted to help him with his new responsibilities. Because Solomon sought God first, he was blessed with more than he expected. As mentioned in 2 Chronicles 1:12, Solomon received both wealth and honor from God. The Lord also allowed Solomon's empire to extend beyond Israel and Judah. Solomon's kingdom stretched beyond the Euphrates River, the land of the Philistines, and as far west as the borders of Egypt. During the days of Solomon's kingship, Judah and Israel lacked nothing. The land was flourishing with crops and livestock. The Bible also tells us in 1 Kings 4:21–25 that the kingdom was secure, and Israel and Judah were also at peace with all their neighboring countries.

In addition, 1 Kings 8:19 says that Solomon was also chosen by God to build a temple. With God's wisdom, in the fourth year of his kingship, Solomon built the most magnificent temple in ancient Jerusalem. Without considering the cost, Solomon used pure gold, silver, and bronze in the Lord's temple. While following God's instructions, Solomon completed the temple in seven years. The Lord was very satisfied with the temple. Second Chronicles 7:15-16 states that the Lord proclaimed the temple as holy. The Lord also said his name would be on the temple forever. Then the Lord made Solomon a promise by saying that he would hear the prayers of everyone who prayed and repented.

Do you believe that the Lord will hear the prayers of the saints? Better yet, when you pray, are you confident that the Lord is paying attention to your prayers? Throughout the Scriptures, we are reassured that the Lord hears every prayer request spoken from our lips. As recorded in 1 Peter 5:7, every detail of our lives is important to the Lord. Therefore, because God is intimately involved in every aspect of our lives, we should accept his invitation to cast our cares on him. That's right: the Lord is waiting for us to surrender our worries and anxieties to him. With that said, the Lord is looking at you, anxiously waiting for you to involve him in your daily activities. When you ask the Lord what he thinks about your situation, you are demonstrating that his opinion matters. However, when you exclude the Lord in your planning, this reveals how selfish you really are, especially when you say you are a Christian. Take a moment and think of a time when your spouse, family, or friends excluded you from the planning process. How did you feel when they forgot about you? If you didn't feel good, then imagine how God feels when you exclude him. The next time you need anything, ask God first. When God isn't disregarded, he will surpass every expectation that you could ever imagine. God's heart is touched when you make him a priority. God's assistance is priceless, and we should never take him for granted.

Power Points on Applying God's Wisdom to Your Life

Proverbs 3:13 affirms that you are blessed if you are in pursuit of knowing God's wisdom. You trust in God's profound knowledge instead of trusting your own intellect or life experiences. This is why your mental capacity is always expanding: because your life is governed by the power of obeying God. As long as you are diligent in applying God's wisdom, you will have everything you need. As a reminder, I have created five Power Points called T.R.U.S.T., which will keep you on track as you continue to seek God's wisdom.

>T rusting and fearing God is the beginning of wisdom. We should make it a habit to seek the Lord's wisdom every day. Our knowledge is very limited whereas God's knowledge is limitless. All roads lead to God. There is no doubt that God is the only way. When we are guided by God's divine wisdom, the outcome is always in our favor (Proverbs 1:7; 9:10; 16:25; Psalm 111:10; Job 28:27–28).

R esist the spirit of wavering. If you are hesitant about trusting God, then don't expect anything from him. When you doubt God, this leads to discouragement. If you're feeling uneasy about your assignment, pray. The Lord will give you wisdom to complete the assignment (James 1:6-8; Mark 11:24; Matthew 7:7-8; 14:31; Philippians 4:6-7; 2 Corinthians 4:18).

U *nique, peculiar*, and *fearfully and wonderfully made* are the words that God has spoken about you. Keeping this in mind, you are set apart by God to complete a specific assignment. You have a distinct talent. God has given you wisdom to create brilliant ideas. Therefore, welcome the divine intelligence of God in your life (Psalms 119:73; 139:13-14; 1 Peter 2:9; Exodus 19:5-6).

S tand firm on what God has told you. Be brave and keep a resilient attitude. A mustard seed of faith is all it takes to believe in God. With faith and God's wisdom, you can achieve the impossible. This why you must believe that you are victorious and never defeated (Hebrews 11:1; Philippians 4:13; 2 Corinthians 5:7; Matthew 14:27; James 1:12).

T urn your ear to wisdom. Learn and listen carefully to the voice of God. When you seek knowledge and understanding, you will find wisdom. Wisdom is a gift from God. Nothing compares to having God's wisdom. Insight, honor, and power are the outcomes of having God's wisdom (Proverbs 2:2-10; Proverbs 3:6; Proverbs 3:13-18; Proverbs 4:22).

5
Secrets to Waiting on God

Wait for the LORD; be strong and take heart and wait for the LORD.

—PSALM 27:14

In Faith, David Waited on God

DAVID'S UNWAVERING FAITH IN the Lord is evident in his writings throughout the Psalms. An excellent example of David's practice of waiting on the Lord is demonstrated in Psalm 27:14. Within this text, David expresses that waiting on the Lord will require faith, patience, and trust. David understood the importance of waiting patiently for the Lord's perfect timing. With that said, because David was a man after God's heart, the Lord chose him to be the king of Israel (1 Samuel 13:14). According to 1 Samuel 16:13, the prophet Samuel anointed David at a young age to be Israel's future king. Yet, David had to endure challenging circumstances before God's promise was fulfilled. Indeed, the Lord is a covenant keeper; at the age of thirty, David became the king of Israel. Thus, Israel had David as their king for many years.

However, David was a fugitive prior to becoming Israel's king. David went into hiding to avoid being murdered. Saul, the king of Israel, was jealous of David and threatened to kill him. Saul's jealousy began when he, David, and the Israelites returned from fighting the Philistines. During the battle with the Philistines, it is recorded in 1 Samuel 17:51 that David killed a giant by the name of Goliath. When the men returned home, the women heard about David's heroic act of killing Goliath. After hearing the good news, they began praising David for his accomplishment. Despite David's victory, Saul became very envious and angry at David for receiving praise from the women (1 Samuel 18:6–8). From that moment on, Saul made many attempts to kill David. Nevertheless, the Lord had great plans for David's life; therefore, Saul couldn't cause David any harm.

Be Patient, God Keeps His Promises

Are you waiting with anticipation for God to do something amazing in your life? I hope so, because God has made many promises to you and to me. If you're expecting God's promises to come to pass, then you will have to do as David did. Through his own experiences, David learned how to wait on the Lord. David did this by consistently placing his faith in God's divine power. Even when the odds were against him, David relied on God's strength rather than his own. Therefore, he was convinced that Numbers 23:19 would work for him. The Scripture explains, "God is not human, that he should lie, not a human being, that he should change his mind. Does he speak and then not act? Does he promise and not fulfill?" To put this simply, when God makes a promise, it shall come to pass.

Keeping this in mind, although man may disappoint us, the Lord remains faithful. His way is perfect. According to Psalm 12:6, the Lord's word is reliable; therefore, he can be trusted. Psalm 119:90 also declares that the Lord's faithfulness is continued from generation to generation. It is also clear in Jeremiah 1:12 that the Lord is committed to keeping his promises. The Lord does this by watching over his word to ensure that it is fulfilled. That being said, we must believe that God will accomplish his promises in our own lives and in the world. On the other hand, if you're a disbelieving saint, then waiting on God will be difficult for you. Unfortunately, Christians like to get ahead of God. Instead of waiting on God, which is critical, we prefer to take matters into our own hands. We must realize that our impatient behavior is offensive to our Father. Having said this, confidence and faith in the Lord is essential, especially if we are going to wait on him.

Taking this into account, if you desire to live a life of joy, blessings, and peace, you must develop the skill of waiting on God. While you wait, instead of worrying about God's response, focus on your family and serve in your church or community. However, don't become so consumed with serving that you neglect God. This is why you must be deliberate about spending time with God. To live a healthy and fulfilling life, we must make time for God. Making time for the Lord clearly says that you care about pleasing him. Consider what Hebrews 11:6 says: a person who sincerely seeks the Lord shall be rewarded.

The Benefits of Waiting on God

Based on what I have previously written, listed below is a brief description of two stories from the Bible regarding waiting. Although the stories are very different, the outcome is the same, which reveals the benefits of waiting on God.

The first story begins with a love story between Jacob and Rachel. When Jacob saw Rachel, he instantly fell in love with her. Rachel was gorgeous. She was the younger daughter of Laban. Laban knew that Jacob loved Rachel. In fact, Jacob wanted Rachel as his wife. In exchange for marrying Rachel, Jacob worked with Laban for seven years. However, not everything went as Jacob planned. After working for seven years, Jacob asked Laban for his wife. Laban told Jacob that it wasn't customary for the youngest daughter to marry before the oldest daughter. Feeling betrayed, Jacob had to work another seven years if he wanted

Rachel to be his wife. Deeply in love with Rachel, according to Genesis 29:20–30, Jacob worked a total of fourteen years before marrying the love of his life.

Have you read the love story of Jacob and Rachel? Isn't their story fascinating? The love story of Jacob and Rachel is an illustration of the endless love that the Lord has for us. The remarkable love of Christ is beyond human comprehension. The apostle Paul reminds the saints in Ephesians 3:18–19 to embrace the magnificent love of God. As we do this, we are transformed to look more like our Father, God. By understanding God's love, we are empowered to live according to his will. We also learn from Isaiah 30:18 that the Lord is waiting patiently to show us his love and mercy. In addition, Numbers 14:18–19 reassures God's people of the Lord's covenant and faithfulness toward us. He is slow to anger, full of love, and is always merciful in releasing us from our transgressions. Now then, let us take the advice of Psalm 118:1 and give thanks to the Lord, because he is good and his love endures forever. Think about this: God's endless love will never change because he is love, according to 1 John 4:8–16.

The second story involves another amazing event within the Bible. This is the story of the prodigal son. The prodigal son didn't want to wait for his father to die to receive his inheritance money. As recorded in Luke 15:12–13, the prodigal son asks his father for his inheritance. Once the son received his money, he left his father's house. Even though the son left home, the father never stopped looking toward his son's return. The father waited and waited, but his son never returned home. Yet, when the son spent all his money and acknowledged his sin, he returned home.

One day, the father saw his son from a distance as the son walked toward their home. Immediately, the father ran toward his son. He hugged and kissed his son and welcomed him home. After the son confessed his mistakes, Luke 15:11–24 describes the father giving the son a celebration party. In this story, did you notice how the father displayed Christlike behavior toward his son? Just like the father of the prodigal son, our Father, God, is always looking forward to seeing his children return to the kingdom. Once we return and confess our sins to the Lord, Luke 15:10 says the angels also celebrate. This example of the prodigal son's return to his father's house is an excellent demonstration of how God loves us, forgives us, and with open arms welcomes us back to his family.

Waiting Acknowledges God's Authority

Despite our difficult situations, we must learn how to wait on God. When we learn how to wait on God, we are following God's advice in Psalm 46:10, in which he says, "Be still, and know that I am God; I will be exalted among the nations, I will be exalted in the earth." This acknowledgement of God's sovereignty indicates that you are giving him total control over any situation that may arise. Habakkuk 2:3 also encourages us to wait on God by saying, "For the vision is yet for an appointed time, but at the end it shall speak, and not lie: though it tarry, wait for it; because it will surely come, it will not tarry" (KJV). Therefore, when you commit to obeying God, you will wait on him to tell you what to do. During your waiting process, also ask God to give you a mindset of expectation. Imagine this: when you have an expectation mindset, you will believe that God will do it. With an expectation mindset, the issue of waiting on God isn't impossible. Therefore, if you remain optimistic, the situation will turn out well for you. Especially if your situation looks unfavorable, you can sit back, wait, and rest in the arms of God. Now then, because you respect the Lord's timing, every promise spoken from God to you will become a reality.

Expect a Miracle

When he heard this, Jesus said, "This sickness will not end in death. No, it is for God's glory so that God's Son may be glorified through it."

—JOHN 11:4

Perhaps you're a person that believes in miracles. In most cases, you understand that miracles are sudden or delayed. However, to believe in miracles, one must have faith. Faith gives us the ability to have hope and expect the best. With an expectation mentality, we are waiting with anticipation for an answer from the Lord. Soon, our excitement will become a reality because miracles usually occur when we least expect them. With that said, Jesus performs miracles every day, whether we believe in miracles or not. Consider this: the very fact that we are breathing today is a miracle! Of course, this isn't something we did but rather what the Lord did for us.

As recorded in the Gospels, many of Jesus's followers believed in miraculous healings. Mark 1:32 reports that Jesus healed many people with all kinds of diseases. The Scripture says the sick came to Jesus in the evening after sunset on the Sabbath in accordance with the Jewish law. Sadly, the religious leaders, also known as the Pharisees, considered healing on the Sabbath as a work-related activity. Do you practice the Sabbath? How often do you spend time worshiping the creator of the universe, God? As a Christian, spending time with God is important. Even if you're not expecting a miracle, the Lord deserves some quality time with you. Besides, practicing the Sabbath will help us refocus and recommit our lives to the Lord.

Due to desperation and expectation, the Pharisees' law couldn't stop Jesus's followers. The people following Christ didn't have a problem waiting after sunset on the Sabbath to receive their healing. By obeying the law and because of their faith, many people received their healing. Are you confident that God has the power to heal you as he healed individuals in the Bible? Think about it: since demons acknowledge God's power, shouldn't you? Luke 4:41 notes that even the demons recognized the supremacy of Jesus Christ. In a loud voice, the demons shouted to Christ, saying, "You are the Son of God." After the demons said this, Jesus displayed his authority by telling the demons to stop talking, and, of course, they obeyed him. Now then, if you are still doubting God's authority, then read your Bible. Reading and studying your Bible is vital to understanding your Father, God. As you read your Bible, your faith is activated, which will help you believe in the power of God.

Waiting Glorifies God

Furthermore, we must be patient and wait on God, the miracle worker. Waiting on the Lord is critical. Your desire to glorify God is demonstrated when you learn how to wait on him. In John 11, Jesus glorified God by waiting on him. Within this chapter, Jesus's beloved friend Lazarus died unexpectedly. Lazarus was the brother of Mary and Martha. Jesus was also good friends with his sisters. Lazarus's sister is the same Mary, according to Luke 7:38, who met Jesus while he was eating at the Pharisee's house. As Jesus was sitting at the table, Mary, also known as the town sinner, approached him. Then she knelt at Jesus's feet and began to anoint them with an expensive ointment. Mary begins to express her love for Jesus by weeping and tenderly kissing his feet. Jesus accepts Mary's worship. At that moment, Jesus tells Mary that her sins are forgiven because of her faith in him.

Meanwhile, Jesus didn't rush to see about Lazarus when he heard the news about his death. Jesus was more concerned about pleasing God. He knew that his friend would live again. In fact, Jesus told his disciples that Lazarus was asleep. Jesus understood that Lazarus's death would bring God glory. As a matter of fact, John 11:6–7 records that Jesus passed by Bethany and returned to Judea to do ministry after hearing the news about his friend's death. Bethany was the home of Lazarus and his sisters. By the way, how do you feel when the Lord doesn't respond to you immediately?

In many cases, we allow disappointment or doubt to settle within us. Unfortunately, we become discouraged, frustrated, or lack patience while we wait on the Lord. Yes, waiting on the Lord is difficult, and it will indeed challenge our faith. Nevertheless, we must learn how to trust God's timing, which is purposeful. As we do this, we can find joy and comfort in knowing that God has plans for us. Besides, when we have faith, we will wait with confidence that the Lord will handle our situations.

Lazarus Is Raised from the Dead

Finally, Jesus returns to the village of Bethany. Lazarus, his friend, was in the tomb for four days. The moment Jesus arrived in the city, both Martha and Mary blamed him for their brother's death. John 11:21 explains that Martha said, "Lord, if only you had been here, my brother would not have died" (NLT). After listening to their accusations and seeing Mary cry, Jesus began to cry. Did you notice the humanity of Christ? Within this text, John 11:33–35 shows the compassionate, attentive, loving, and gentle side of Christ. Neither Mary nor Martha understood why Christ took his time to see about their brother. Christ waited to return to Bethany because he knew that Lazarus would receive his healing. Although Christ was grieving, his confidence in God's power didn't waver as he went to his friend's tomb.

While at the tomb, Jesus begins to pray to the Father and commands the spirit of death to let Lazarus go. With unwavering faith, like Jesus, we can also speak life into any situation. Therefore, if we believe, anything is possible, as we can see from the story of Lazarus. Consider this: the words we speak hold immense power and will have a profound impact on our lives and those around us. As Proverbs 18:21 states, the words we speak can either bring life or cause destruction. By choosing to communicate with words of love, hope, and encouragement, we are creating a better future for ourselves and for those we care about.

Further, Lazarus immediately rose from the tomb after hearing the voice of Jesus. There were also a number of Jews who followed Mary to the grave site. Can you imagine the faith of the people who witnessed this incredible miracle of Lazarus being raised from the dead? After Jesus brought Lazarus back to life, John 11:45 says that many people believed in God! This shows that our actions and behaviors can influence others to turn to God or turn away from God. Therefore, we must be mindful of how we conduct ourselves when we are around individuals who don't believe in God.

The Lord once again displayed his miraculous power when he raised Lazarus from the dead. Just like Lazarus's illness was not fatal, our Savior knows that our situations are not detrimental either. As you can see, we can have an incredible experience with God, but we must have the courage to speak to him about our problems. It's important to remember that God is always there to listen and guide us. Better yet, we will see extraordinary things happen to us and around us when we learn how to trust God. Therefore, let us remember the words from apostle Paul in Ephesians 3:20: faith is needed if we expect God to do the unthinkable.

Furthermore, have circumstances or people prevented you from fulfilling God's call on your life? If so, ask God to remove any obstacles or people that will keep you from accomplishing his will. Think about this: without faith and an unrepentant spirit, you will abandon your assignment. However, if you stay committed to your assignment and remain true to your values, you will avoid aborting God's calling on your life. While fulfilling your assignment, keep in mind that the Lord is not about complacency but progression. In other words, the Lord is always moving forward, making sure that you are fulfilling his purpose. With God's help, you can strive towards making a positive impact in the world. As a result, you should be inspired because the Lord has empowered you to achieve great things that you didn't believe were possible. This is why we are told in Proverbs 2:20 to follow the path of righteousness. When we do, Proverbs 13:21 proclaims the righteous will be rewarded. On the other hand, if we choose another path, Proverbs 13:13 says whoever doesn't obey the Lord's commandments will surely live a life of destruction.

God Is Pleased When We Believe

Lastly, to believe in God's miraculous power, we must be persistent in asking God to renew our mind. When our mind is changed, it is impossible for us to doubt God. Once our mind is transformed, we will experience God's power. Even when our faith wavers, we have the number-one best-seller, the Bible, to help us with our unbelief. However, it's up to us to believe in the Holy Scriptures. When we choose to believe God, we will worry less and expect more from him. Furthermore, when we have expectations of God, we are not worried if our prayers are not answered immediately. Instead, we will view our unanswered prayers as being postponed rather than denied. Having the faith to wait on the Lord also says that we don't underestimate his power and authority. As we patiently wait, we are looking forward to experiencing a mighty move from God. Therefore, when God speaks, we will quickly obey his voice, as Lazarus did. With that said, we are confident that God will be glorified no matter what he decides for us!

Power Points to Waiting on God

The benefits of waiting on God are inconceivable. Learning to wait on the Lord is one of the most important things you can do. Your dedication to the Lord is evident when you patiently wait on him. This also says you respect the Lord's timing and opinion because you know he is right. Therefore, your relentless and determined spirit to please the Lord will not go unnoticed. Listed below are four Power Points called W.A.I.T., which will be helpful while you wait on God.

> W aiting on the Lord will prevent you from taking unnecessary detours in life. When you wait on the Lord, this allows him to control the situation completely. This also says you understand how to be still in God's presence. The Lord honors your waiting; therefore, you will flourish in his kingdom (Acts 1:4; Psalms 37:7; 40:4; 62:1–2; 115:14; Isaiah 30:18).

Anticipation says your faith isn't wavering, nor are you complaining while you wait on God. You understand that waiting is a part of God's plan. You inspire others with your optimism and resilience. In fact, your enthusiasm reveals that you're hopeful although you don't see God's promises. That being said, your confidence in God has led you to believe that he will respond (Psalms 37:4–6; 40:1; 130:5; Joshua 1:3; Romans 8:23–25; Proverbs 28:20).

Intimacy builds your relationship with God. Intimate moments with the Lord will also build your faith. As a result of this, the Lord will confide in you because you are his friend. As a friend of God, you will learn how to rely on his knowledge, not your own. When you depend on God, you can be certain that he will lead you in the right direction. Because you waited, the Lord will equip you with power to overcome any challenges. He will also bless you with peace and joy (John 5:15; Proverbs 3:5–7; Psalm 5:3–7; Jeremiah 29:11–12; Exodus 20:8; Genesis 8:8–17).

Timing of God is always perfect. His thoughts and ways are so much higher than we could ever imagine. Therefore, put your hope in the Lord, who knows everything. Divine insight and strategies are revealed when we wait on the Lord. As a result of waiting on God, your bright future awaits with endless opportunities. Fear God, believe the impossible, and you will be a change agent for the kingdom of God (Proverbs 13:22; Isaiah 55:8–9; Psalms 33:4; 37:34).

Bibliography

Cox, Jeff. *From Vines to Wines: The Complete Guide to Growing Grapes and Making Your Own Wine.* 5th ed. North Adams, MA: Storey, 2015.

Taylor, Norman. *Taylor's Encyclopedia of Gardening: Guide to Ground Covers, Vines and Grasses.* Boston: Houghton Mifflin, 1987.

www.ingramcontent.com/pod-product-compliance
Lightning Source LLC
Chambersburg PA
CBHW071743090426
42738CB00011B/2544